UnLocKiNG THe ExITs

POEMS BY ELIOT KATZ

COFFEE HOUSE PRESS

MINNEAPOLIS, MINNESOTA

AUTHOR ACKNOWLEDGEMENTS Thanks to the editors of the following journals and anthologies in which some of these poems previously appeared: *Aloud: Voices from the Nuyorican Poets Cafe, Long Shot, The New York Quarterly, IKON, Cover, Paterson Literary Review, Big Scream, Sunflowers & Locomotives, Nada Poems, Napalm Health Spa, The Underground Forest, Digraphe, Booglit, In Defense of Mumia, Education for the People.* In addition, variants of four early poems are reprinted here from out-of-print *Space and Other Poems for Love, Laughs, and Social Transformation* (Orono, ME: Northern Lights, 1990). Special thanks for manuscript suggestions: David Cope, Alicia Ostriker, Deborah Pohl, Allen Ginsberg, Andy Clausen, Danny Shot, Kathy Crown, Eric Drooker, Allan Kornblum, Janet Jones, Bob Nasdor, Sarah Fox, Bob Rosenthal, Stephen Bronner, Johanna Lawrenson, and Chris Fischbach.

Coffee House Press is supported in part by a grant provided by the Minnesota State Arts Board, through an appropriation by the Minnesota State Legislature, and in part by a grant from the National Endowment for the Arts. Significant support has also been provided by the McKnight Foundation; Lannan Foundation; Jerome Foundation; Target Stores, Dayton's, and Mervyn's by the Dayton Hudson Foundation; General Mills Foundation; St. Paul Companies; Butler Family Foundation; Honeywell Foundation; Star Tribune Foundation; James R. Thorpe Foundation; Pentair, Inc.; the law firm of Schwegman, Lundberg, Woessner & Kluth, P.A.; and many individual donors. To you and our many readers across the country, we send our thanks for your continuing support.

Coffee House Press books are available to the trade through our primary distributor, Consortium Book Sales & Distribution, 1045 Westgate Drive, Saint Paul, MN 55114. For personal orders, catalogs, or other information, write to: Coffee House Press, 27 North Fourth Street, Suite 400, Minneapolis, MN 55401.

LIBRARY OF CONGRESS CIP INFORMATION
Katz, Eliot.
    Unlocking the exits : poems / by Eliot Katz.
       p.   cm.
    ISBN 1-56689-079-0 (ALK. PAPER)
    I. Title.
PS3561.A753U5   1999
813' .54—dc21   98-23484
                                                 CIP

10 9 8 7 6 5 4 3 2 1
printed in Canada

CONTENTS

DINOSAUR LOVE

On the Museum of Natural History's 4th floor
I greeted my old friend:
"Hey, T. Rex! Long time, no see!"
My buddy flashed his killer teeth:
"Over two years, E. Katz,
I missed you."

Surprised, I asked, "You missed me?
I didn't know dinosaurs had emotions.
Rexy, did you know love?"

Rexy sighed: "I knew love
    not as humans can
but as humans do:
    love of self
    and love of finding something weaker
        to pounce upon.
E. Katz, can your species be saved
    by love's possibilities?"

"Rexy," I answered, "you haven't lost
your ability
to ask the tough question.
Let me ask you something we humans
have been curious about for centuries.
How did you die?"

"I don't know.
One day I looked around
and I wasn't there."

—1986

ODE TO THE CAR KEYS

In the late sixties we were so fed up we wanted to destroy it all. That's when we changed the name of America and stuck in the "k." The mood today is different, and the language that will respond to today's mood will be different. Things are so deteriorated in this society, that it's not up to you to destroy America, it's up to you to go out and save America.

—Abbie Hoffman, National Student Convention '88 ,
Rutgers University

In a burst of Dionysian FRIGHT
    you're snagged
        keys locked inside
            first week first car in 16 years
forced to ring a stranger's steel curtain door
    for a healing coat hanger never used before
        dipped in 19 consecutive generations
            of herbal locksmith experimental libations
but the magic potion hanger won't fit
    in the window
        till you rip rubber insulation padding
            and then doorknob comes only halfway up
then back all the way down
    50 times
        halfway up and all the way down
            till finally you realize this ain't gonna work

So you call local police for help
        but begin screaming
            "You broke Martin's new plastic jaw
                with a Jim Crow hangman's billy club law!"
then casually describe your local campaign plans
        to institute civilian review board rock & roll bands
            that would include 6-year olds
                with no corporate two-party political bias
so by the time you ask
        about getting car door opened
            all officers are busy
                and locksmith equipment all locked up
Just in time you remember a spare key
        in your bedroom dresser
            hid in pages of an old spiral notebook
                you haven't looked at since heavy drinking days
but you realize apartment's an hour away
        and front door keys
            on your car key ring
                with six others
now easily countably floppy in the ignition
        O keys, how brilliant your bright sunned reflection
            through the passengerside window!
                O shit

No wonder 16 years without a car
        and today at work I'm driving
            an 8-months pregnant homeless Latina woman
                to look at apartments
She hasn't had house keys for awhile
        and O My Keys she's getting nervous
            having contractions while I'm only
                learning to deliver messages

but she knows he's coming early
      "it's a boy" her last boy early
          one before that too
              she might have liked a girl
they'll be no more apartments to see today
      that she can't have
          despite shiny new
              Section 8 rent subsidy certificate
and only 5 more student loan repayments before
      eligible for new loans to paralegal school
          where she'll study to lawyer
              once she finds a legal home
and you my car keys are in their proper place
      the ignition
          but the path is blocked
            & I can't reach you
no matter how I open
      cleansed perception
          to Blakean infinity
            of blue skies above

Yvette feels guilty
      doesn't want any Amandla Crossing
          Transitional Housing residents
            to hear of my screw up
'cause they'll think her bad luck
      so I yell second time today:
          "Don't internalize everything! It's all me!
          I'm Fucking Idiot for the Day
this's absolutely no reflection on you!"
      to no avail
          she still doesn't want me telling
            and I feel guilty for losing my cool

till she says at least I'm acting
    human now
        not like some ice cube social worker—
           role reversal—here—midstreet
wherever we're stuck
    with keys where they're supposed to be
        but not now please O keys not now
           please not now not now not now not now
not not not not not not now now now now now now
    hypnotized into iron trance
        depressed about red tears
           dropping my palm's longest line
who would believe our story
    when no more than two senators
        expressed belief
           in Anita Hill?
Magically suspending disbelief
    doesn't cut
        the mustard tree
           of earthly political justice
and now a right-wing Supreme Court zealot
    can help illustrate that ideology does not know
        rigid ethnic or gender boundaries
           though sociopolitical power
up to this historic point mostly does
    If Anita Hill wasn't believed
        what woman will?
           Surely not 27 homeless women
in our transitional housing program
    sure not 50 kids
        with homelessness
           carved into cranial histories

Yvette's worried, supposed to be back soon
     to take her two kids out of daycare
          where we left them with 48 others
               about to throw 250 million p-i-e-c-e-s
of a giant jigsaw puzzle
     of the world or country or state
          can't remember which
               onto the floor
Now that I think of it
     it looked
          a lot like
               the American left
or maybe Picasso's *Guernica*
     as seen by Gert Stein
          after reading *Ulysses*
               and deconstructing the Cyclops chapter
Yvette's supposed to be back by 5:00
     my watch stopped at 4:30
          does that mean I can't be late?
               O my bright shining keys! o my!

Things could be worse!
     I could be writing an ode to my clothes
          standing naked here in Woodbridge
               groping for an anti-Enlightenment
edenic fig leaf technology
     while Neruda gets angry with me
          for ripping off his ideas while failing
               to move the planet noticeably forward
I could be waving pro-choice coat hangers
     as lone protection from extremist explosions
          of toxic-dump land
               to radioactive air missiles.

I could be Father Aristede
    given unceremonious boot
        by U.S.-trained gun-toting cahoots
            while unknown mystery beings
who look just like Tonton Macouts
    in nonhuman-dimensional suits
        disappear organizers against coups
            before teary-eyed silent infant cries
Before Yeltsinian greed took over
    Gorbachev thank Compassion's Window
        returned for a moment
            from his long coupy trip
I condemned that one
    right away
        no more antidemocratic acts
        in socialism's name!
The dream of a utopian left was
    to lead Democracy's child
        into new & underground parts
        of the city
not to try saving the city
    by offering the child up
        as sacrifice
        to the latest books
turned into the latest
    manufactured biblicistic fractured
    tylenol tablets
        Tip those KGBCIA statues over!
America I've given you all
    and now what & where am I?
        With the key thru the window?
        And no one to drive the car?

Over half our Canadian neighbors
　　live in provinces driven
　　　　by democratic left NDP
　　　　　　while here ozone layer disintegrates
& any tourist can smell
　　rotting perfume riding NJ's Turnpike
　　　with car windows open
　　　　　Where's our New Democratic Party, my keys?

I measure every grief I meet
　　with probing eyes wider
　　　than that slot
　　　　between window and locked doorknob
here with me is a woman talking to death
　　saying no, I survived your phantoms
　　　saying my kids and I
　　　　will beat you to the wheel this time
and looked at this way
　　car keys don't matter
　　　what kind of metaphor
　　　　is this?
what the ability to drive a machine
　　compared to this?
　　　how the literary canon
　　　　stand up to this?
what kind
　　of home
　　　is getting into a car
　　　　anyway?
Yvette:
　　"What, you suddenly have goddamned
　　　time
　　　　to daydream NOW?"

And I laugh
   caught
      in the lack
         of act
thinking how beautiful it would feel
   jingling keys
      in my palm's
         eye again
After the modernists deconstructed
   what that exists
      and postmodernists added questions
         of identity construction & appropriation
to the equation that could never be
   an equation to them
      O reasonable unreasonableness
      who am I
at this moment to them
   this only jewish child
      of a concentration camp survivor mom
         depression-pinched chemistry dad
now helpless outside a locked car?
   Who is this pregnant homeless woman beside me
      whose name I have changed
      to write this poem
now trying her luck with the door?
   Who is that kicking her belly
      to enter this polluted world
         before it's ready?
Who are these survivors
of domestic violence, of injuries
that suck up the
rent, teenaged mothers kicked

out the house, drugged out escape
routes, AIDS ripping
apart growing bones, father-in-law
rapes, local police
badges branded on their bodies, 27 different
unaffordable reasons for homelessness, ten thousand
reasons for the kids, without
playgrounds, tumbling on used heroin
needles, bunkbed torched by racism's adult
white gasolined robes, dinner sacrificed
for parental addictions to
theft of convictions, congress-dictated plutonium
profitable neglect, 3 A.M. drunken bangings
on cardboard welfare motel doors, rusty handgun barrels
armed & aimed into
the cradle's third eye, thunder lightning
of 100 million multinational sexual
abuse nightmares, it's over it's over it's over it's over
there just ain't no reason for hope it's got
to be over;
    no I refuse
       to give up
         hope
got to get those keys
    without breaking
      the window
         one can't buy a new window
50 kids back home working on a jigsaw puzzle
    half african-american, one-third latino
       one-third white, one-quarter indian
        one-tenth amerasian

and one more tenth
    born into pneumonia's
       infant mortality
         death grip
O endless ironizing detachment into an ineluctable void!
WHO IS GONNA HELP THEM PUT THOSE PIECES TOGETHER?!
O keys! Got to get you soon
without breaking the window O world!

    ——1991 — 92

THESE HANDS——A PRESENT

I held out these hands
that have worked and loved
and offered them to Despair.
No chance, Despair calmly replied,
> *if I know you,*
> *in another minute*
> *you'll find hope.*

So I razored a few fingers
and held out the bloody offering
toward Hope:
> *Your gesture is kind*
> *but it's too easy an out*
> *you're lookin' to find.*
> *I cannot create a sure thing.*

I clasped my hands together
and offered the package to
Truth, who grabbed 'em gloating:
> *I gotcha now!*
> *First I drain the blood*
> *then hand you over*
> *to my messenger, Death.*

Oh, shit! I yelled when the blood
was down to the last drop; and
    I got my hands back just in time.

Whereupon, I took a pen
and with this verse
    I give these hands
        to you.

—1984

TO THE VEGETABLE AISLE

Under refrigerated water spray all looks healthy,
romaine, red & green, boston bib, watercress—
        how choose a lettuce?
How to know which of you has natural soil's nutrients intact?
Hey arugula! Why haven't I seen you here before?
Who let those prepackaged sick leaves in the door?
There's plenty broccoli bunches, no ketchup—
        at least the Reagan/Bush era is over!
Which squash has more vitamin A? Spaghetti or butternut?
        Would one of you please raise your label?
Speak up! Which of you has been microwaved?
Who here likes Creamy Italian?
Who's not afraid of the juicer's steel blades?
Brussel sprouts and red cabbage, settle your price wars
        peacefully.
Chestnuts, are you a vegetable now?
Ah tofu, you are the cure for famine & carnivorism.
No wonder u.s. wants yr French soybean subsidies cut!
How juicy these ripe Jersey tomatoes
        lulling me for an illusory moment
                this really could be a garden state.

Wait a minute now! Why isn't this aisle as well lit
      as the candy bar section?
Why a Mars bar cheaper than a bag of spinach?
Doesn't it cost more to grow a candy bar?
When a six-year-old child I remember watching
      a professional wrestler described
            as having a "cauliflower" ear.
Cauliflower, it was 20 years before I could look at you again.
Actually, for a long time in childhood I refused
      to eat vegetables.
It was a way of rebelling I think.
Later, I substituted alcohol for not eating vegetables.
Now I welcome you radical & mostly sober escarole & chicoree
Now kale, now garlic, now red peppers & parsley.

Peas & green beans, who will protect you from being canned
      and frozen to death?
Without values of internationalism & democratic accountability
      in all public institutions
            who will safeguard the diversity?

Who protect us from irradiation & pesticide?

Who will assure the right to organize?

Who sets transnational standards of minimum wage, ecohealth,
    & safe working conditions?

Who make sure hypertechnology doesn't take over?

After a right-wing tide, who will remineralize your soil?

Who will assure access to your aisle for all?

Who will apologize for bumping my cart into shoppers
    while writing this poem?

Sleep tight, don't let the bacteria bite—

feed the struggle for another night.

—1992

WHAT NO GOD KNOWS

Even as I declare there is no god
a subconscious one-eyed monster digs its bloody teeth
    into my lower back to protest.
Most times I know that notions of who knows god best
    have been responsible for human slaughter
    equaled only by racism and ideas of private property.
Yet, I can't help remembering age 16 with table tennis
    tournament matches tied
    21-all in the final game
I'd often repeat to myself:
"Please, god, help me win this one, just help
    me win this one."
Maybe the mantra relaxed me?
I won many of those games.
I also lost a lot.

Why anyone supposed it evolutionary
to move from many gods to a stern one
    I'll never know.
At least before we'd been encouraging debate
    among the gods of lightning and greenery!

We are all people chosen to make this world
    a better place!
Isn't that right, whoever or whatever radiant
    being, nonbeing, or infinite emptiness
    might be listening?
Hear O Israel! What Lord says: democracy for all,
    end the occupation and develop
    two-state cooperation?

No god knows what god would do!
No god knows why gods come and go!
No god knows what no god knows!
No god knows why it's up to us!

—1988

WHEN YOU DRINK SO MUCH FRIDAY NIGHT
SATURDAY NEVER ARRIVES

That doesn't happen.
Saturday always comes after Friday.
Though sometimes
    you're not there to see it.

Like when your date
is in bed in the other room
    with a guy who doesn't drink so much.
Do you think you're not being witness
    makes it less so?
I say when the tree falls
    it falls
    whether you get hit or not.

Like when Rusty Staub homers
to win the game, bottom of the ninth,
    two innings after you've fallen drunk
    under your upper deck seat,
add one in the "w" column for a Mets win,
    and you "Washed out in need of rinse."

Like when you're fired
    for sleeping on the job.
Though you don't wake for the message
    you've got no vacation pay coming.
I say when the laughter ends
    it ends
    whether you hear or not.

—1986

GULF WAR CYCLE

—⚷—

PUTTING T-REX IN MOTHBALLS

"It's not fair to the other kids
that they won't be able to see it
    for a long time,"
seven-year-old Frances told *The Times.*

Old friend, they're putting your 4th floor
    museum home
to renovative rest.
For next five years,
    even your rebuilt fossil'd bones
    will appear extinct.

Rexy, I never even got a chance
    to wave good-bye.
I'm sorry as a sorry human can be.
What happens here
    o'er the next five years
    I'll detail when next we meet.

Right now, heading into 1991,
a bloodthirsty America threatens
    a despotic Iraq it used to prop,
which now occupies Kuwait
    and threatens Israel,
whose right-wing government
    takes it out on what should be
    a free peaceful Palestine.
Saudi Arabia, Syria, and Turkey win more
    weaponry'd prizes
    with each dissident they break bones
    & throw away the name.
In a region of too much repressive rule,
there is boiling hot sand
    in monarchy's mysogynist shoes
& national gates are wallpapered
    with missiles nuclear and chemical.

Sixty miles north of Los Angeles
record snowfall has ruined this year's
    citrus crop.
Here in Jersey it's 60 degrees Fahrenheit
    two days before Christmas.

Some say global warming's arrived;
      others say the dawning of a new ice age.
Either way, military wallpaper hasn't done
      the trick.

Sylvia of Brooklyn with son and grandchild
told *The Times:* "Just look at that beast.
It dwarfs us, but we're smarter
      than it ever was."
Rexy, how dare she call you a beast!
Now, in this poem, I once again stand up for thee!
There's no evidence thus far in Mesozoic fossils found
      that you thought nuclear ecological disaster
      would turn back at the border!
Rexy, I wish you didn't have to leave.
I'd tell the curator if I could
      to put those smelly mothballs
      in the mothballs.
If I never see you again,
better luck
      the next round.

ALTERNATE ROUTES

They're talking tomorrow in Geneva
but it's impossible to know
      whether Baker or Aziz
      will be listening.

The French want to negotiate
an international Mideast peace conference
        held out as olive branch
        for Iraq's withdrawal from Kuwait.

Germany agrees with the French
and it's Germany's oil
        the U.S. is dying to protect.
        No matter—Bush isn't talking sense.

Bush has finally asked Congress approve war plans.
But a WPIX psychologist historian insists
        any real debate will be watched
        as weakness by Saddam Hussein.

If there's war, the American press has been told
there'll be no photos of injured allowed
        and all press reports will be censored
        by oxymoronic Army Intelligence.

The army command assures that antiwar sentiment
won't be x'ed out
        and past history predicts America's mainstream press
        will censor itself without much help.

Despite horrific repression, Bush armed Saddam against all
reason—& now refuses any compromised nonwar alternatives.
        Bush's all-or-nothing thinking would be called
        denial-filled psychosis on any analyst's couch.

Whether by ethics or realpolitik inspired,
it's time to debate the drive to war
        and to build an impressive antiwar movement—
        since there's no couch big enough for 10,000 quacks.

CONGRESS CARTOONS DEBATE

None are real.
The voices are Daffy Duck meets Elmer Fudd.
Skins made of cardboard.
The wooden dummy's lips are moving.
The tinman has no heart.
A necktie on a real human could never be so tight.
They decide the fate of nations yet not one
    can pronounce Saddam's name correctly.
They've studied Orwell enough to know the antipodean equations:
    war is peace
    and ignorance is strength.
None ever die in wars.

PRAYER VIGIL

Demonstrate—and generals tremble
Organize—and borders collapse
March—and feet get wet in the Ethical Lake
Resist—and Earth becomes the Golden Realm

SUPPORTING THE TROOPS

Go troops!
Go c.o. troops!
Go blow your nose over an underground stove, troops!
Declare your conscientious objection
    to this war for oil and royal retention!
Tell your captain you refuse to fight the bad fight!
You have more important things to refuse to die for!
Go home quickly before the u.n. deadline passes
    and danger arrives!
If you're still in the u.s., go troops, quickly
    to a draft counselor!
Call 1-800-86-NO WAR, troops
    for the best legal advice no money can buy!
Just say no, troops!
Save your ass from Bush's new gas, troops!

PEACE MEETING

At Central Jersey's peace coalition meeting,
    we agree: No war & yes kindness
    for u.s. troops—bring 'em home
but most other demands endure heated debate:
Whether to call for ending sanctions economic
    (not until Iraq leaves Kuwait;
    u.n. injunctions only way avoid war)—

whether condemn Saddam along with Bush
      (of course)—
which already-split national march to join—
Have those who brand poems
      as "politically correct"
      or "preaching to the converted"
ever been to an organizing meeting?

—⚷—

AFTER BOWLS & POLLS

While many United Statesians wonder
      whether Simms or Hostetler
      will quarterback next year's Super Bowl champs,
professional pollsters say most Americans
      watching TV's Space Invaders videogame flashes
      support Bush's war.
My own poll, which includes those without phones,
      is more evenly divided
and reveals many Americans also believe
Cruise Missiles travel faster than sound,
      then stop
      at the front door
knocking politely so civilians can leave
before explosions create mile-wide craters
      where neighborhood children once stood.

The *London Guardian* relayed Turkish news reports
    of 150,000 Iraqi casualties
    after one week
and Nimr Madi and other refugees describe to papers
    lonely roads
    of chauffeur-driven corpses.
u.s. television media doesn't even ask
    about Iraqi casualties
and still doesn't know any Iraqi names
    but for one
and they can't seem to pronounce his.

Scott Specher was America's first pilot shot down.
A navy comrade remarked: If he's dead
    it's because God needed a copilot.
Bush brings Billy Graham to his bedroom
    and announces pray-for-peace day
as u.s. pundits wonder aloud why Saddam
    would fight a "holy war."
According to Pentagon and press,
    the peace movement is marginal
    and missiles "patriotic."
No major u.s. anchorperson seems to notice
    1984 jogging backwards just around the corner.

It's hypocritic to decry an ex-Bushite's aggression
as the world's largest power
    bombs new cratered pages
    into *Guinness's World Record Book of Wars.*

Even King George would turn in his dethroned grave—
watching blood spilt in bucketfulls
    to defend Saudi monarch's misogynist streets
    and public square beheadings for dissent.
The Gulf's fish and gulls could use a rinse
    but will have to wait their turn.
When the ground war begins, and bodies—
    disproportionately Black and Latino—
    fly unceremoniously into hidden graves
    in a fenced-off Dover Delaware yard
next year's NFL season won't matter much
and the larger-than-reported antiwar marchers
    will grow beyond continental bounds.
Nobody likes a general, Republican, Democrat
    or NBC news anchorperson
rubbing electric bootheels into their eyeballs
    night after TV *Nightline* night.

BOMB SHELTER BLUES

Five hundred children, women, & elderly men
    killed in a Baghdad shelter,
which by all major media assumptions
    was really a military command center—
since Bush's gang by definition
    would never aim at civilians
despite all the evidence one sees
walking Port Authority Bus Station's basement.

ABC *Eyewitness News* takes it to New York City streets
all 4 Americans interviewed shrug shoulders—
    no regrets; human ashes just part of a just war.
It's tough to know where to point the camera lens:
When the news skims off dissent
    it's a heartless film which floats to the top.

THE COOKING SHOW

Defense Secretary Cheney says it's unacceptable
to allow Saddam the possibility
"to rearm and, rather than spend
the nation's wealth on improving
the circumstances of his people,
rebuild his military machine."
What chef worth their cayenne
would not recognize
an American recipe?

WELL DONE

With Iraqi troops attempting to exit Kuwait
& the figleaf cover of war's rationale shed
Bush has ordered
    continued
        tanktread slaughter.

Since TV's corporate pundits have proven capable
    of mesmerizing
        America's yellow ribbon majority
such naked viciousness provides quite
    the popular thrill.

As war now approaches its bloody close
America's free press applauds the defeat
    of our "Vietnam Syndrome."
Once again the USA can bomb
    without televised guilt!
Now war at any cost!
Once more we can give war a chance!
Finally, we can find our favorite
    high-tech weapon
        on a Topps trading card!
Soon the United Statesmen of Bechtel
will get back to work
    rebuilding oil-filled Kuwait
        for a slick price.

POST-WAR CULTURE

Gilgamesh
succeeded
in his spiritual
quest
&
returned
home
tired
&
thirsty
for
a
Pepsi Light.

—1990 — 1991

YOUNG EYES OF PARIS

The youth of France
are excited for the possibility
    of awakening the sleepy democratic left.
In America we struggle
    to make the possible
    seem possible.

    ——1991

YVES TANGUY PAINTING

Once we leapt out the water
today the water
    can't get us out.

    ——1991

TOMBSTONES

In Paris's most famous cemetery
Francis Combes points out the tombstone
    of a "minor French poet."
No reaction
    from the poet.
It's amazing how little
    the dead fear.

—1991

PÈRE LACHAISE

Walking thru the cemetery
a young American asks us:
    "are you looking for Jim?"
"No, we like Jim Morrison
    too much
    to wake him;
we're gonna try to wake
    the communards
    instead."

—1991

TOULON

In Toulon, French Riviera,
topless men & women
     tanburn under sun's casual rays.
A navy submarine chugs
     past shore
          clicking sharp iron teeth.
Seven wind surfers
     coolly clear out
          of its path.

—1991

SAVED

On Norman's coast
America helped save France
     from the Nazis.
Today America's helping
save France
     from the French.

—1991

THE CLOCK

France is six hours ahead.
The U.S. can never seem
    to catch up

    —1991

THE GLOBE

Which corner of the Earth
    are you from?

    —1991

A NEW MORNING WARNING POEM
FROM THE CHICKEN POX COOP

Blistered fevered dizziness rising
    & falling one week now—
it's intellectually crystal clear as fashion mag's
    touched-up photos
how skin-deep beauty's a self-esteem soultrap
and yet, emotional acne-recalling depression's depths
    enter my few stand-up moments
as this newly bearding & poxing face becomes more
    & more unrecognizable to the bathroom mirror.

O what can I say to you who nurses me through
    chicken pox & broken car door locks
who brings me food even in weak moments
    when I get rude too hung up
    on acting with certitude
to receive your gifts in the unnegotiated way
    they are intended.
I suppose I have found it easier proclaiming to the planet
    how much about my life & this world
    I have learned from you
than to quietly accept these quiet moments
    of unconditional love.

I have always been better at giving than getting
        better at forgiving than forgetting
better at feeling guilty about debts
        than at collecting on my bets
as a child often wanting to give parents back the gift
        of a life before mom & her family
        cattle car'd to Auschwitz's torture & death camp:
the gift, of course, no one could ever give back.
Now in adulthood, what do I say to a giving companion
        other than I am so thankful for your love.

But my partner hasn't had chicken pox yet
        so must sleep on futon in other room
        while I lie in bed feeling quarantined
with not enough strength to sit up
        more than 10 minutes at a time——
only little reading, little writing, & lots of TV
        watching the bombing over Baghdad continue.
Even Maya Angelou's powerful condemnation
        of "armed struggles for profit"
couldn't stop our young sax-playing prez in new role
        as rock & roll hawk

and couldn't even remain a poetic protest vessel afloat
against the narrowing tide of a "free" cement press
    describing it solely as a poem "celebrating"
    the richness & diversity of America.
These blisters on my face keep breaking out
    as those blistering bomb craters break in:
War is not inevitable:
Many who get it once in childhood
    refuse to get it later in life.

How to make sure newly energized counterculture
    doesn't become the new air cover
    for new U.S. air wars?
    What to do now while world's newest baby boomers
    scoop drinking water
    from bombing's pockmark'd puddles
and play with neon uranium shells littering
    Basra's Made-in-America cancer playgrounds?
Once we've been shown even a great public poem
    can be made to stand alone
    what do you, I, we do now?
O Beauty & Truth! How I too would love to celebrate
    but from this sickbed the altering eye alters
    all DC celebrations to make them look sick!
Look at Les Aspin & James Woolsey up there under TV lights?
Can't every television viewer see those chicken pox?
Hurray the Bush that burned us all has been dethroned.
As Abbie Hoffman once said, better the lesser of two evils
    than the evil of two lessers.

Christine's favorite bumper sticker said:
    "Clinton will make you sick; Bush will kill you."
From this chicken pox coop, I'd say that bumper sticker
    was one hell of a prophet.
As I swallow 2,000 more milligrams of vitamin c
    I know these chicken pox will soon heal
but what medicine will it take to heal this
    still-sick DC bunch?
To watch a real unselfish love become possible for all?
To end this, yes, bombing for profits?
To end this rape, this racism, these ethnic cleansing camps?
To make my job working with homeless families forever obsolete?
What brand of oatmeal bath did that doctor say
    would rid the body
    of this everpresent itch?

—1993

IN THIS FAILED DEMOCRACY

I placed my soul in a brown shopping bag,
    poked around the corners for my own awareness—
      then placed it open, below her eyes.
It wasn't enough to win her trust—
    even with a naked soul at her fingertips
      she couldn't quite distinguish my ingredients from the rest.
It's a brutal patriarchy out there—
    any man or woman who doubts that is an idiot:
      A heartbreak doesn't change the social facts.
The mystery is what to do with a caring heart
    in the meantime—the time between the world mean as is
      and the world we mean to become.
Like the Bonus Army I came veteran'd to heart's capital expecting
    hard work's rewards; and was turned back by strength
      only Emotion's most decorated generals could muster.
She mistook parts of me both for those who'd been rotten
    to her, as well those who had been super nice
      to her best friends.
But I was me—not any others in this failed democracy.
    The mystery—what to do with a tired heart
      in the meantime.

—1993

WHO DOES WHAT TO WHOM

These questions of who does what
  are of little import now—
the facts are we continued to have a great public life
  but our private one began suffering
   & you had the courage to leave.
Why the top floor of trust wasn't fully constructed
  after seven years
   no longer needs answer.
Who was more stubborn about what,
  who was sufficiently expressive, sufficiently kind,
   patient joyful spontaneous, future-oriented in the present—
who withdrew too easily & often, snapped too quickly,
  raised voices in harsh tones, grew silent to punish—
   many interpretations can now remain open.
You about whom I would never utter
  even the slightest negative estimation
   had the courage to move first
and tonight the moon is three-quarters full & low
  in the sky, ready to be nuked out of its magical
   realist existence at a moment's notice.
Like your green velvet hat trying to communicate
  to my blue and yellow plaid scarf—sometimes patterns,
   that should keep adding up, don't.

It is a new year. Throughout the globe are boiling new wars,
    deathsquad skeletal remains, missile-launched putsches,
        nuclear brain tumors, corporate-designed electroshocks,
frozen homeless limbs, buzzsaw eco-murders,
    neo-fascist soldier rapes, televised infanticides,
     poked eyes flying past 10,000 stations—
& you and I: Now from separate rooms & separate streets
                      we will both speak up.

—1994

YOU THINK THINGS ARE BAD?

They could be worse.
You could be a life-like
Museum of Natural History model
of the last
Two-Ton Prairie Buffalo
frozen forever
with a parasitic insect pest
nesting in your furry brow
agoniz-
       ing
to
      evolve
         finger-
           nails
to scratch
      that unrelenting itch.

——1994

ODE ON MELANCHOLY
WAVING GOODBYE
—*for Deborah*

I had given my romantic fortunes
    up & over
to the red wine glass's
    sole remaining sip,
to the TV detective show's last
    suspenseful blip,
to the organic apple's
    last sweet crunch.
I had given up & over,
    over & up,
when into my life you walked
    brown-eyed & frizzy haired.
It was a postmodern artistic bop
    & I remained unsure
whether this walk
    was destined
for fleeting sidewalk moment
    or near Eternity.
After all, I had dreamed
    a tuburcular Italian room
where lost loves
    wither away,

where the urn's unfinishable
  embrace
seems preferable to Joy's
  momentary grape.

But each successive night
  bore new surreal light
and every new embrace
  shuddered
this mid-aging body free
  into expressionistic glee.
Goodnight, for now, old poets
  of melancholy yore—
For luck's ominous draw
  might just seed
magical redwood trees
  as well as globed peonies.

——1995

BEHIND THE CURTAIN

Ah, my new love, we finally did it in the shower—
  after a week of too many volcanic crises,
of too many 6th grade arms torn out the sockets, too many
  youthful families sleeping under winter's bridge—
yes, there is another way—beyond the rusty claws
  ripping purple veins out teenaged chests;
beneath the two-hundred-ton fingers of shame
  poking around the neglected dead;
at the calm foot of silent screams burning two thousand
  years at one monstrous stake after another;
through the Armor of Caution that looks backward all day
  wishing only for a disaster we can duck.

Ah, behind your beautiful soapy skin, your body
  perfect against mine, your long wavy hair
in my eyes that for this moment see no trouble—I will become
  any musical instrument you would like to play.
Like this, catastrophe halts at the shower curtain—
  moving like this, how can anything go wrong?

—1996

THIS PAST DECADE AND THE NEXT

I inherited the tempestuous
>
> energy
>
of fighting
>
> against the fascist encampment
added a pinch
>
> of elegiac feelings american
& minstreled
>
> my interplanetary songs
>
> up & down the Raritan
to help radical
>
> democratic Poetry's
>
> spirit
>
> > & body
>
> swim
>
> in this modern concrete city.

The town changed
>
> though not
>
> > as I'd intended.
Joyce Kilmer's tree
>
> grew upside
>
> down.

Teachers skipped
       over the sex ed chapters
    in their Johnson & Johnson
                 history books.
The Environmental Protection Agency's
         Unidentified Flying Watchdog Copter
flew backwards
      & its razorblades
broke thru
         New Brunswick Cultural Center's
   painstakingly stainglass'd
     exit door.
Torn black T-shirts were hosed
            then hung
   to dry
      on silvery grey police hooks
    to pay for crimes
               typed out
    behind faceless video screens.
The weekly Town Meeting
        became
   the Town Hiding Place.

I flipped my mirror'd
    sunglasses around—
           no help.
I started pulling out my gray
     hairs every morning
   before work—
           no help.

I dunked my designer sneakers
            into the dirty riverbank—
    only left waterlogged
                 footprint puddles
      over all where I'd been.
It was hard to reach
        the Bush White House
from where I stood.

I quoted from Coleridge's notebooks
           on the mechanical nature
   of imposing
      a predetermined form.
I escaped to my rooftop
     & screamed
           romantic poetry epithets:
"Empire is no more! and now the lion &
   wolf shall cease."
"O, weep for Adonais—he is dead!"
"I sound my barbaric yawp
      over the roofs of the world."

My MTV neighbors went crazy
    & started aiming
surreal threats
     through institutional window blinds

till I fell quiet
            remembering how
        the Philadelphia police
                        rained red white & blue
liberty bell bombs
                down MOVE's newly unsound
        oratorical head-
                            quarters.

What was there
        left
        for a Hub City
                        poet to do?
                D.C. was guarded
        by asphalt circles
        the New Jersey
                    Turnpike couldn't touch.
            Even New Yorkers
                            and Lost Angels of the West
            didn't give a shit
                            about us.

I'd already dropped off
                reflections of
        the living
                    & dead
        down at Melody Bar's
                    Nostalgia Dance Benefit For The Future
        and the city's xenophobic
                        .boundary patrol

had confiscated
       & iced
   my next-wordly
     11-dimensional paintings
               on nonmaterial canvass.

I thought to give up
   lay down
            go right to sleep
wait for sexy utopian dream
     to get me through
   next day's nightmare,
but mom's concentration
      camp inheritance
kept me awake
   like unbreakable toothpick guardians
   keeping watch
          over my lids.

So I kept at it
    getting up & falling
up & falling,
      and getting up again
   if for no other reason
        than the ethical question
   of knowing
          no other way
    to live.

I vowed to keep
        test firing new
               & experimental
    rocket pages
          one right after another
     till I hit upon the one
              to take off
from this real world
    I have worked like my scientist
             father
     to understand
 & fly
     in a billion different
         poetic directions
    like a heat-seeking daisy
              wheel
     searching for the next.

—1991

GREG'S NEW HIDEOUT

Here lies one from Hub City's heyday
who with gray-streaked mustachio'd swaggery style
lived five years past a step ahead
the Rent Collector's acidic dead bolt smile.
One who lived in cars abandoned
turning ignitions till an engine sparked—
winter heat a lottery prize parked—
has died atop night auto's runny hood.
For two weeks none could i.d.
who was he
took a last decapitated bow
to show what the hell
lurks outside a welfare motel.
Be rest assured
it's he in dying
raised a rearview mirror
revealing temporal desire's
    ten dimensions
        failing to materialize
           & far from home.

—1991

WHAT THE WOMAN
IN THE PASSENGER SEAT SAID

"My mother brought me up to believe
    you were a punk
if you used a weapon
    instead of tearing someone apart
      with your bare hands."

——1992

TO THE NJ
DEPARTMENT OF HUMAN SERVICES

"Outrage and possibility are in all the poems we know"

—Muriel Rukeyser

Four hundred humans
      cram Newark City Hall
   for your hear-
        ing
              on new welfare regulations
which limit benefits
       for single "employable"
    individuals
            to six months out of the year
Fifteen thousand humans statewide
   70% black & latino
       35% women
    will be scis-
                sored
     from computerized General Assistance rolls
        on January 1st, 1993
Happy New Year
      one more good day
              good night
  good-bye

to another tumultuous American year
                    and to about eight thousand humans
who will lose
            emergency shelter placements
    and apartment rent subsidies.
How many amputated
        frostbitten
                            limbs
    will litter the bushes
        of 500 New Jersey city halls?
How many shivery dreams & frozen screams
    interrupted and stored
                        in 6-foot thick
        ice cube tombs
            never to thaw
                    never to get cracked alive
    from some cryogenic suspended
        animation pistachio shells
    two centuries later
            by future Star Trek generations.

C.D. at the mike—age sixty—from Newark—
                    sleeps in a 10-bed shelter
    after waiting over an hour
                        on line
when 50 more young guys
    join the line January 1st
        C.D. wants to know
    how will an older guy get in
            even if he's first on line?

"What you see before you"
        C.D. declares

                        "is the first casualty
                of these new regulations."
Humans in the audience clap & cry

                                it's both intellectual
                & visceral now

        why

                people really are gonna die
which is one thing I say in my testimony

                                a few hours later
                but now C.D.'s holding up

                        his blood pressure medication
he's considered "employable"

        cause he takes these two pills

                                        4 x daily

        but once cut off welfare

                        no more prescriptions paid
                & he'll go into a deep sleep

                                in less than one week
without trial

                without the 5-10 years of appeals
                        he'd get if he shot someone

Why are your representatives
        sitting there
        such expressionless
                        beaurocrats

All the cards are on the table
                and they're turning up
                            without much ambiguity
Over fifty people have spoken
                none in favor of this new Cruel of Law
A diverse group of advocates
                and welfare recipients are here
        where the first seed of
                media-covered public outrage
                is planted
and many of us realize intellectually
                            and viscerally
        this is not a door
            that will open because
        the magic reasonable password
                        has been spoken
            but it's now
a political battle
        that can
                be won.

DHS, let's put a little spring
            in yr safety net
                instead
    of cutting
            the chords
        & letting the bodies fall
                    directly
                            into their graves

or leaving their $140/month

        paper money behind

               & going directly to jail

                    the only warm bed in town

With the momentum we win here

              we will address

     why so many

       are fall-

          ing

              onto your rolls

                  in the first place

How many ice ages

       before the next species calling

    itself human

    arises from a Big Melt

  to provide

        something it can call

              "human services"

   without lowering its eyes

               in shame?

——1992

AN EMPOWERMENT PROJECT
—*after Gregory Corso*

On a right-wing radio talk show a caller asks what "empowerment"
    means—everyone is using the word—is it a commie coup or
    should true patriots use it too?
Listener, don't accept other people's words unquestioningly—
    especially right-wing talk show hosts—use empowerment
    in your own sentence
Write about gooey empowerment or meatfree stewy empowerment
Or: It's ten o'clock, do you know where your empowerment is?
How many around the world lack empowerment?—Can you present
    your answer in postmodern multimaterial collage?
Disempowerment isn't funny but to survive you sometimes have to
    laugh about it
Gregory C. thought an autochthonic poetry spirit empowered a
    nonviolent revolution in America: He was right—until
    Reagan smiled years later for the six o'clock news
After a long work day, TV anchor smiles give me a deep sense of
    loss, how about you?

Boris Yeltsin has undemocratically disbanded parliament—Russian
    Constitution says VP Rutskoi takes over—Rutskoi, who has
    advocated democracy, takes his presidential oath—U.S. officials
    & western press laugh at Rutskoi's preposterousness—
    which side is empowered?
In former Yugo, it seems none ever have enough power & none in
    power is empowered to stop power-seekers from massacring
    & mass raping those without power
Aristede was elected Haiti's highest accountable power but like
    Thomas Wolfe can't go home again
The Israeli-PLO peace agreement could be beautifully empowering if
    those who signed are really empowered
Valorie Caffee beating Jersey's legislative Lynch machine would be
    grassroots-movementy empowering
Working through childhood grief take-a-deep-breathily empowering
Andy Clausen's next book taking off futurismically empowering—zaum!
Mandela free in cheering Yankee stadium was unprecedentily empowering—
none are empowered until all empowered—does anyone seeking
    power today believe this?

I was always too shy to say how I felt about those in power until
    through poetry I got empowered
Turn the power back on so I can remember what it is I'm so hot about
Shit, sometimes I feel it's a hell of a fucked up world & I'll never
    feel empowered
maybe knowing that there's no sure way of knowing what will happen
    next is empowering
Is liberation theology, goddess philology, or god-is-dead more
    empowering?
At least half-a-dozen TV preachers forgot to put the 'e' in god-is-dead
maybe new gods and no gods need to work on personal growth issues
    at the same weekly therapy group?
maybe all this talk of democratic power is a cruel hoax?
Why is that baby's plate empty? Amandla—who would play such a joke?

——1993

LOSING NIRVANA

Youth dies daily
a new airplane loses a wing, a young guitar breaks a string
a makeshift cardboard shack collapses on a family of four
it's always too young to die homeless under HUD's awning
or with a bullet through the neck on the street or in bed.
When they say to stay indoors or they say to just say no
the young see right through their hypocritical fucked-up polluted fuzz.
Who are they who say these things?
It doesn't always matter . . . they're there.
Youth dies daily
yet somehow the death of artistic talent strikes the heart point-blank.
I watched MTV's all-night tribute, he was up there with Morrison it's true.
A purple atomic cloud explodes from unknown origins
fiery daggers pop up every 2 minutes from unpredictable sidewalk cracks
invisible death gas awaits job seekers in stuffy boardrooms
a brick wall built segregates each human form from another
the world keeps coughing coughing coughing yet refuses to clear the smoke
but young artists desperate for enlightenment see through it all.
Through it to what?
It doesn't always matter . . . there is a there—
which inspired song alters
despite the daily drudgery and beyond the senseless dying.

—1994

FOR MARK BRADLEY,
SONGWRITER & CHEF

Walt Whitman is crying.
One of his greatest and most grateful children
    has been taken
    far too early.
Beyond nihilistic smokescreens and MTV's glare
    of celebrated self-destructiveness,
a few visionary potentials commit their lives
    to figuring out this world
    to change it.
In only 28 pre-aneurism years, Mark had learned
    to bake food and cook lyrics.
But when this world refused to budge,
    his heart left
    to transform the next one.

No—in the death of the young, metaphors
    are never so clear
and fluke tragedies never made sensible.
Sometimes poems are helpless—
    he should never have died,
    this youthful American bard to come,
this bountiful songwriter who actually lived
    according to his song.

Mark was Hub City's Phil Ochs
      with electrified vocals.
He helped lay bricks along the trail
      to Baldwin's fire next time,
revived Plath's most upbeat measures,
      & set Shakespeare's sweet bird song
         gently upon eternity's high-tension wires.

O Cathy, though there is nothing we can do,
      ask and we will do it.
Death, prepare an angelic pillow for this soul
      who ought to be a stranger to you still.
Mark, the promise I made to Walt
      at his Camden grave
I make to you—my young friend, poet-brother,
      artist extraordinaire, soul of righteousness—
Down with the multinationals!
Down with their A & R robots with rusted ears!
We will make sure your song is heard!

      —1994

BLUES FOR THE MOMENT

In modern France the right has won
Farewell our coolest monuments
Go wash the dust off sophist reason
Farewell dear Enlightenment

Dear Kant, your grapes have soured
Hello atavistic rhymes
Farewell to more inventive critics
Marx you've died yet another time

Even Zeus seems too progressive
For these days of severed nations
It's a crime to want no borders
Or to strike for a human face

Goodbye Slovakia farewell Russiadream
Not enough coats anyhow
Goodbye Rwanda Oh well Bosniascream
Shrug yr shoulders curl your brow

Now it's LePen & now it's Duke
Zhironovsky & Milosovic
Now it's Newt poppin' out the frying pan
Ain't it a laugh, ain't it a stitch

So it's back to blood and back to soil

Farewell our modern monuments

To the corporations go the spoils

Farewell dear Enlightenment

——1995

MCNAMARA'S GHOSTS

The Best & Brightest were neither
It wasn't only a Battleship they steered wrong
They looked up at Dawn's Slippery Sky and cried "Ours"
Thought a nation's most sacred trees could be tortured into spying
Feared the Creaky Springs of Youth more than Napalm Rings of Atomic Warplanes
Loaded up Heroin Haystacks with Hidden Needles, created Dr. Paranoia with injection
    of Bad Magic Breath, & described the Wide-Eyed Corpse as a drop in the hour's
    popularity poll:

If history's lessons are now all learned, why Carnegie's hired soldier-ghosts still wearing
    steel-toed boots to bash in living skulls?
Four decades after "Howl," why croaking Moloch of heavy judgment & skeleton treasury
    still worshipped as Angelic Guardian of Father Knows Best Family?
Why Tantalus still sacrifice his DeVine child & assemble Archivo death squads to grab a
    few runaway Arbenzian banana republics?
Why Urizenic newspaper of record Editorialists always so righteously angry thirty
    years too late?
Why is it still so fucking tough to be poor in America—is it New Deal or Civil War
    those robber-baron phantasms want to fight over?

Ah, citizens slouching toward 500 TV channels, isn't it fun watching our retired execs
    rip out their apologetic livers?
Isn't it cool to hear McNamara's melting historical sax moaning a true blues riff?
Got to admit, it's cool, it IS COOL! knowing even McNamara's samsara
hangs out looking looking looking for forgiveness & love!!!
Okay, now can we apologize to Vietnam
for the 3 million dead?

——1995

OKLAHOMA CITY

I wonder where a Gulf War vet
might get the ridiculous idea
that you can solve all yr problems
w/ bombs?

——1996

LESSONS FROM AN UNEASY CHAIR

Through a hazy cloud of violence begetting violence;
amidst confusion of unseen shooters vanishing around thick-aired alleyways;
among a swirl of random bullets ricocheting off unknown origins;
between an emergency room bedside nonconfession nonrecalled for two months
& a gas station owner's nonexistent narratives shredded & tossed into
    a homicide detective's disintegrating can;
only the state executioner's clear desire to murder stands tall & indisputable.
Here lies a robeless hanging judge;
here a fraternal disorder of police;
here autochthonic tragedy gives birth to social calamity;
here the young learn how meaningless a thoughtful life appears still on the
    post-Cold War screen.

From this chair lessons look easy:
flick a switch or lethally inject—
then put yr feet up
& watch another nation fall.

        —1995

A NOSE FOR BLOOD

Incorporeal shadows around the redwood table agree:
    the Poor Department has too many toys—
        the War Department not enough.
So they're building a fortress brick by bar,
    plutonium radioactive tube
        by compacted chemical sludge cube.
Grumpy Gramm's shadow is grouchier than Phil—
    head to foot without a midsection,
        eyesockets deprived of sunlight too many years.
Dollop Dole's specter is ever scrambling
    for a more comfortable position at the table—
        which it refuses to acknowledge as a table.
Newt's ghost is shrewdest & knows historically
    newts have come & newts will go—
        but knowledge doesn't a feeling nor action sew.
Centripetal Bill's apparition stays put longest,
    asking the tough existential questions
        before caving in.
These shadows have developed a nose for blood—
    among this group, only the redwood table knows
        where in the empire sentience dwells.

—1995

THIS LOTTERY'S FIXED

They're ending welfare
    as they'd like
       us to know it
          so erma's name comes up
       a million times
    then lockheed
gets the million bucks.

   ——1995

FROM THE DEPTH
OF THE DEPTH OF THE ABYSS
—*after Paul Eluard*

From this exhausted seat, the faces are difficult to discern,
eyes formless and hungry,
brave hands of the dream strewn about unseen.
It is darker beneath this flag than in that world lit only by fire
where Charlemagne and his soldiers of Christ beheaded 4,000 Saxons
  on one eclipsed morning.
Now the monsters carry long lethal needles.
The radioactive plague moves stealthily here.
On these shores, contagious rain washes out even the cruel joys of fire.
So why do the dragons of holocaust never sleep?
Why do the pterodactyls even bother to sharpen their claws?
Which of these lovesick cushions conducts the fatal jellyfish jolt?
With a lit match, shadowy figures begin to emerge—
without startling new ideas, I'm afraid those hands will no longer be enough.

  —1995

THE BACK SIDE OF THE PAINTING

Walking the Louvre isn't the least bit daunting.
Who cares if one makes it into all the rooms?
Michelangelo's slaves look like they want to break out of the place anyway.
Prud'hon's angels of justice look quite human.
LeGuide's Cupid brings a monkey and dog together, so who can envy the
        human couples their good fortunes?
Salvator Rosa has stuck his horses' asses out at heroic battle's unsuspecting viewers
(how many warloving visitors have been mooned by Rosa's 17th century steeds?)
and Prestinari's 1600 Adonis is 10-feet tall and well-proportioned, but nevertheless
        has these funny red spots on his white marble dick.
I have to get back to work, so trip to Paris will be short.
But what are those red spots on that penis, I wanted to ask before leaving?
        1600 art or 1995 art terror?
Have Ronald McDonald's ketchup-splattering tentacles reached this far into France?
Or is this Adonis alive & growing nakedly revealed personality streaks?
Is this why Venus de Milo has thrown off her arms?
Is this why Delacroix's bare-breasted Liberty is taking the lead?
Is this why the Mona Lisa wears a bulletproof vest?

——1995

EDISON POST OFFICE, NIXON BRANCH

At Edison Post Office, Nixon Branch, I ask smiling gap-toothed clerk for a self-stick
     book of stamps
and am shown two kinds under counter: mixed fruit and American flag.
Is this a trick question? If I pick peaches & pears, will they bury my letters in an
     unmarked Kalamazoo grave?
Is there an abandoned building near Chicago 68's convention filled with unopened
     envelopes from those who chose fruit?
Will midnight telephone rings tell me student loan repayments haven't arrived?
Will postmasters open my poetry submissions and steal my best lines?
Suspend my postal privileges 'till I agree to lick the stripes' back side?
Until I place it right-side-up, with a pledge and a prayer?
What would the clerk say if I leaned over counter & whispered lovingly into his ear:
"but I'm in Abbie's corner, believe in taking the flag, not burning it"?
Nervous about consequences, I nonetheless announce in loud voice: "I'll take the
     mixed fruit!"
Then silence, a shuffling of fast hands—receipt, change of a ten, book of stamps, all
     in one hardly visible motion—
I say "thanks, have a nice day" and look at his brown eyes staring beyond, watching
     wintry outdoors turning slowly into spring.
"You never know . . . " he answers, "Next!"

—1996

ONE OF THESE YEARS

It's a new year. A two-story homeless tent's been pitched along
    the Raritan River's New Brunswick side.
A new congressional hellhound rips triangular chunks of flesh
    off the fed's already skinny ankles.
Because of early east coast snows, everyone around my building
    is walking sidewalks of thin ice.
Last month a train-stopping strike bug hit French workers and
    college students;
more than ebola, Corporatism's barbwired heads are hoping
    to prevent this bug from reaching American shores.
Where I work, more children are finding their next nutritious meal
    tougher to find—
so the stock market rages beyond monstrous expectations.
It's slippery outside & the wealthiest winds are grabbing more slices
    of the gaunt earth.
One of these years, someone is gonna take a hard fall.

—1996

MAD COW DISEASE

I ran into a cow who was so mad
he was roaming across the field screaming:
"I will be eaten by humans no more!"

—1996

OLIVE TREES

The olive tree spreads its wide Italian branches.
    Out of the soil of no-hope,
        hope springs.
Bombs fly over Lebanon.
    Jackie O's underthings are auctioned.
        My refrigerator grows a weird mold.
An open eye sees through closed lids;
    a thorny rose repairs a flooded garden;
        a sugarless cake sweetens heaven's new gaze.
The ashes of the dead swirl—
    we hold our hands out, palms up and open,
        grabbing the best ashes we can.
We never know if we'll get another chance.

   —1996

THESE TWO HANDS

These two hands slap each other silly
rub fingers into palms in deep heat massage
pound fists into blushing delirium
intertwine pinkies for a sacred earth vow
swear devotion with prickly sacrifice
crack middle fingers' weary angry knuckles
dig at pain's pressure point in the "v" where base of thumb
        meets start of forefinger
come together in full-clasped imploring union
rest meditatively quite separate and apart
patiently stretch each other's fingers, each one, one at a time—
these two hands: these two dynamic hands.

—1995

ON THE REBOUND

In Europe the left is on the rebound
the soul too
    rebounds
to where?
    to where it rebounds
good thing
    before they engrave
        a corporate name into yr forehead
I'm in an Edison motel
    escaping termites
        & termite exterminator fumes
how to mix insects & economies—
    heaven's untold secret
        haunting NYC's smoke-filled cubes
but on the new steel spoons
    of Jospin France, Labor U.K.
        Olive Tree Italia
the blues confess
    they have heard enough of the blues
        for the moment
goodbye blues
    goodbye midnight truckload morphine news
        bye Newt

the Happy Wanderer too
    can figure out
        how to squeeze in a tune
hey ha ha—somewhere's an invisible trail
    lit & ready
        for yr soft walk

—1997

ELEGY FOR ALLEN

Ah, Allen, you gave America a new shape & now you've lost yours
what a long accomplished road it was from the bridge o'er Paterson Falls
through San Francisco's Six Gallery, Prague's May King, Pentagon exorcisms,
    mid-America's Iron Horse, Chicago '68, Jessore Road, Rolling Thunder,
    Rocky Flats, cosmopolitan greetings from NYC's East 12th street,
to heaven, the bardo, a grasshopper, a gray void, the place where all things
    wise and fair descend, the end of suffering—wherever you are,
    the most curious place in the universe.
Yesterday in your new Lower East Side loft, I held a clear plastic bag
    with your ashes inside, fine off-white powder, only a few small bone
    fragments visible, boxed inside last Buddhist shrine.
O those armor-piercing eyes will look out tender photogenic skull no more!
What happens to us? When did we begin taking this trip from energetic
    body-souled beings traveling the world for democratic freedoms
    and dream-forged poetries
to old-age liver cancer bodies lying softly on hospital cots near busy city
    windows, searching one last glimpse of old friends & sidewalk lovers,
    devoting life's last energies to finding new ways to breathe?
Why the hell did we accept this ancient bargain? When did we sign
    this horrific contract for a few mere decades of joy?

Well, you were always discovering a new breath, a new spiritus, a
     no-money-down person-to-person compassion,
now millions across the globe are chanting "ом" in your honor,
now you've joined Shelley's children of light, become a portion of the
     loveliness which once your presence made more so.
But, Allen, how you hung in there! How you gave them hell over four
     decades!
How you bowled over *Howl's* critics piercing thy innocent breast!
How you practiced sanity, candor, intelligence, kindness, and boundless
     imagination as your weapons!
How you mixed humor and information, utopian yearnings and minute
     particulars!
How you extended and subverted literary traditions in the most interesting
     ways and never tired of formal inventiveness!
How you revealed the academy's shower-curtain'd secret: poetry could
     be relevant to our lives!
How you taught all nations' youth to dig through the deadwood of
     exploitation and hypocrisy!
How you were expelled from Prague & erased off primetime radio!
How you showed that a lone human voice well-honed and courageous
     could challenge a multinational corporate bureaucracy!
How you became an Unacknowledged Democratic Conscience
     of Cold War America!

Allen, you made me laugh a New Aware Laughter for 20 years I knew
    your work and you.
I don't think you would have remembered where we met.
Danny Shot & I were sitting, 57 Guilden Street, New Brunswick porch,
    one fall afternoon 1976, awaiting your night's event.
A cab pulled up to Kevin Hayes's apartment across street, you hurried out,
    unloading cardboard boxes from trunk—
your father's manuscripts stored years at Rutgers Alexander Library.
We went to help—your friendliness astonished, I'd just read "Song
    of Myself" & "Howl" first time & decided try poetry—
in one of your last poems you asked for remembrances like this—
With Danny & Kevin, I drove you back to Manhattan that night, you
    threw out empty food wrappers & newspapers from my
    lemon orange Vega,
then took us on a radical auto tour of historic East Village.
Months later, you answered letters Danny & I sent, took ten lines of my
    manuscript—using cross-outs, exclamation points, a few words,
    a reading list, taught my first poetry lesson—
the postcard Danny'd received weeks earlier still implanted in memory—
    each line shd have wit, humor, imagery, perception, double-meaning,
    a new way of seeing or Poesy in it.
In 1980, I apprenticed with you July at Naropa—in '82, you gave poems
    & funds to help Danny & I launch *Long Shot* magazine,
you encouraged my poems the next fifteen years—
even after that 1986 early morning Naropa panel where, hungover
    & nervous, I called some of your famous poetfriends crazy.
These last two weeks, thousands of poets in dozens of countries have
    told tales of your meetings,
Allen, you were loyal & generous to friends & future generations.
Lucky for the planet your words live on—

Lucky for those not yet born *Holy Soul Jelly Roll!* still carries your
    baritone voice,
your blues & holy celebrations grab onto mind's lining and refuse to let go,
your meditative consciousness sits a crosslegged raven on our shoulders
    while we scribble odes & design activist modes,
urging us to write what we saw & rally out of kindness.

What a beautiful new loft you bought, how sad death arrived just a few
    months after you moved in: high ceilings, room for your office and
    your stepmother,
clean kitchen for macrobiotic scrapings, wallspace to frame all yr futuristic
    portraits—
two bathrooms, bookcases galore, prophetic volumes lining shelves from
    polished hardwood floor how many hundreds of feet up to the soul's
    exit door?
Oh Allen, you've finally joined Walt's side amid the enduring dead, how can
    that be all bad?
Now you can forget daily terrors, quit worrying which nation's elected leader
    the CIA will topple during new terms of presidential denial,
which activist friends will be jailed, which youthful heads will bleed from
    Tompkins Square Chicago L.A. Moscow Peking police nightstick,
    where landlords' eviction armies will helicopter next.
Like Blake's Los you gave form to Human Error, Moloch the heavy judge,
    Plutonium's devouring ghost lingering a quarter million years,
    Unchecked Capital's skeleton sweeping homeless off the street,
now it's up to those with flesh on bones to tame our monsters, inside and
    out, to carry your sexy wheel of syllables into peaceful battle
    for the next millennium.
Death's phantom steeds have taken one more wondrous singer—one more
    sweetest wisest soul of all our days and lands—to who knows where?

Praised be the cosmic mystery,

Extolled the enlightened fire which outlives the initial spark,

Exalted the echo which rebounds through the universe,

Blessed be these tears, the tears on cheeks of millions who touched your soft
    hands, your glowing aura, your living voice, your ink'd page, your
    Shambhala coffin.

Allen, you tired your heart lungs liver running years up a zillion flights of
    creaky lower Manhattan stairs—

I don't know what happens after death—just that whatever's been written
    is wrong—

Wherever you are now, I hope it has an elevator.

   —1997

JOSEF SAID

I tell Josef that Prague seems a symbol
    of a nation exploring a path
between an authoritarian form of communism
    and unchecked capital's greed.
His eyes look up: "we would rather be seen
    as people trying to live our lives."

    ——1997

SPRING AT KAFKA'S GRAVE

This first Prague spring day, 1997, is cold as hell.
Here lies Kafka, along New Jewish cemetery's first row.
His neighbors are quiet now, no longer spying.
Here is a beautiful old city lying somewhere in the middle:
between an obsolete map and who-knows-where,
between tough windows and delicate concrete,
between words that have lost their meaning and stray referents
     scrambling for a new sign.
Most have forgotten their Russian, and there's fewer
     English-speakers than rumored.
Whether to join NATO is a no-win choice—
Here lies a nation becoming symbolic against its will.
May life's absurdities continue,
but may they become slightly less painful.

—1997

LIBERATION RECALLED

I

O what heavenly mess we find on earth today! O divine poverty
and fright! From which flowery seeds did such crime and disease
spring? Walt Benjamin wrote that the angel of history faces the
past while propelled toward the future. The wrestling match for
history's meaning takes place past present future at once! But what
if the match is fixed? What if the rules have been encrypted and
locked in secret CIA vaults? What if the contest has been usurped by
carnies dressed in xenophobic costumes screaming into micro-
phones on Saturday morning TV? What if the angel's neck got
twisted this past decade? What if 1990s angel is two-faced? What if
the winds stopped blowing from back to front and now swirl? What
if the ultrapoststructuralists are right and history no longer a
totality of continuities and discontinuities, but now isolated sea-
shells we pick at random self-interest on any clean beach suffering
only mild decay? When does spring arrive then? In 1933, propaganda
chief Goebbels pronounced, "The year 1789 is hereby eradicated
from history." Twelve years later, it was put back into the texts—
from two fronts. Can you find it?

2

—Mom, tell me about your family.
—We were in our family ten people.
In 1944 Hitler came into
Hungary and we lived in a city
called Oradea Mare-Nagyvárad.
We were a family of ten, eight children
and my parents, six girls and two boys. I
was the oldest and the youngest was
about three years, two or three years. And when
Hitler came in, what he did, in a very
short time, he created a ghetto. All
the Jews had to go in one place to live.
What they did, the Germans, they took out all
the Jewish people from one district and
then they took out gentile people from
another district. The gentile people
had to get out of that district and they
put in the Jews there. And they put in one
room two families. Our neighbor was a
family of ten and we were ten, so
20 people were put in one room. And

there was no furniture. The room was all
empty. It was a bit of a big room
but we almost slept on top of each other.
And the kids had to sleep there. My parents
had to sleep there. And we lived in that ghetto
in that house about three or four months.
—This was in Hungary?
—That was in Hungary, yes, in '44.
—Tell me if any questions I ask, you
don't feel like answering.
—Right, go ahead.

3

After a holocaust, who counts the breathless bodies
        lying shackled
        beneath slaveship floorboards?
Who invents theory justifying tourists' annihilation
        of a newly visited continent's
        outstretched-hand inhabitants?
After a quarter of its people x'd out by u.s.-backed
        Indonesian army, how many American PhDs
        can even find East Timor on a map?
What recovery path will end the full-spine shivers
        at the word "soviet" felt
        by so many who believed in utopian ideals?
After the extermination of European Jewry—
        after this holocaust—how does one
        learn to sing in a shower again?

4

—What did your parents do?
—My father, Elias, was a businessman
dealing with fruit, wholesale fruit. And my mother,
Freida, stayed home because she had kids, almost
every two years another baby.
—What about your sisters and brothers?
—We were eight kids. I was the oldest. Three
of us survived Auschwitz and were always
together. The younger kids they killed in
Auschwitz the day they took us to Auschwitz—
there was Etu, Bila, and Tsira, the
youngest kids, and then we had two brothers,
Srul and Mandy.

5

Everything one sees in this world comes from complex interrelations between
    subjective impulses, shared social experiences, and ideas gleaned from
    those that seem the most sensible thoughts studied up till now—
O ye long lines of lyric bards from whom the stuff of delightful dreams and
    nightmares are made, where in this thixotropic ecocidal post-post-post
    emergency room ward does one find the Solidarity Wing's concealed exit
    door to sneak a glimpse of cleansed imagination's Radiant Orchard reality core?

6

—What did you like to do as kids?
—We all played soccer in school. That was the
most popular game in Europe. And we played
with buttons. We had no money so we
played with buttons, and we used to cut off
buttons from the clothes so we had buttons
to play with, which was fun.
—When you were young, did you have political
interests?
—No, never. In that time, as I remember,
Jewish people couldn't vote so nobody
was interested in voting. But I
was always outgoing. I always tried
to fight, bringing money into the house
even when Hitler didn't let us work.
So one time a German person went out
and asked my father if he has big girls,
if they would like to work, and she would teach
them a trade. It was a woman. My father
says yes, I have 12, 14 year-old kids.
And if you wanna hire them, go ahead.
So they brought us there to this lady and she
taught us how to do dresses with a machine.
Hands and knitting things. And right away, just
one time she showed us and we did it.
—When did you and your family first become
aware that the Nazis were coming to power?

—Probably in 1935-36.
The Jewish people couldn't have a radio.
So we used to gather in a gentile house
and they had a radio. We weren't
even allowed to listen to it but
we—one person—always stayed in the street
watching, and we listened to the foreign
radios to see what's going on. And that's
the way we found out how the Jews were going
to be persecuted and what they're doing
in Russia, and the Germans getting ready
to take over all these countries. And that's
how it started, the pogroms. They called it
pogroms. Then the gentile people who lived
there already with us treated us very
badly. We were afraid to go out, and
then the Jews had to wear stars, a Jewish star.
—And what were some of the responses to this?
Were people trying to organize or
did forces seem too powerful?
—No, my brother Altasrul—they got
organized, the kids, the boys. And we were
in Hungary and the borderline between
Hungary and Rumania wasn't
too far. And then the kids got together
and they took other Jews across the border,
whoever wanted to run to Rumania.
And then my brother came back. And sometimes
he wasn't home at night and said he was
at his friend's house. But then he told the truth,

what he did with the other kids, crossing
the border to Rumania. Because
on the border nobody was shooting
yet. The border was open. So one day
he came home and he said to my father:
Let's pack and run away because they're gonna
kill the Jews. Let's go to Rumania—
because Rumania didn't let Hitler in
so fast. In Hungary, they called him in.
But my father didn't want to run away.
He was afraid they were gonna shoot us
on the way. Where can we go with ten people,
8 kids? But Srul says: I just took other
people with 10 kids—and not just one
family. But my father always was
afraid. And then he said, okay, you're not
going out of the house no more. Srul said,
Look Dad, I'm gonna run away and I'm
not coming back and I'll be in Rumania.
He wouldn't even let him out the house.
He wouldn't let him do that. So we all
came into Auschwitz. Because it went so fast.
—Did you ever hear what happened to those
people who were sent into Rumania?
—They probably lived. They never had a
ghetto.
—So your brother helped save a lot of people?
—Yes, yes, yes, but we still don't know what happened.
Then later on, near the end, some people
tried to run to Israel—but the English

people controlled Palestine and they stopped
those people. They wouldn't let them go there.
So they shipped them God knows where. So it
wasn't easy.

7

Speaking to ss leaders, Poznan, October 4th, 1943, Himmler:
"The ss man is to be guided by one principle alone: honesty,
decency, loyalty, and friendship toward those of our blood,
and to no one else. What happens to the Russians or Czechs is
a matter of total indifference to me. . . . Whether other peoples
live in plenty or starve to death interests me only insofar as we
need them as slaves for our culture. . . . I want to tell you about
a very grave matter in all frankness. We can talk about it quite
openly here, but we must never talk about it publicly . . . I
mean the evacuation of the Jews, the extermination of the
Jewish people. . . . Most of you will know what it means to see
100 corpses piled up, or 500 or 1,000. To have gone through this
and—except for instances of human weakness—to have
remained decent, that has made us tough. This is an unwrit-
ten, never to be written, glorious page of history."

To defy Himmler and bring history's secrets
    into animated light:
        does this build empowerment
alongside the overwhelming anguish
    from which one never
        fully recovers?
Should we remember Julius Streicher
    whose posters proclaimed
        without modern hesitation
"The Jews are our misfortune?"
    Wilhelm Marr, 1879 founder
        of pre-Nazi League of Anti-Semites?
Lanz von Liebenfels, 1901 author
    of *Theozoology*—founder
        of Aryan cult worship?
Does it help prevent future repeat to recollect cascadingly
    those who laid the asphalt path
        to annihilation's ovens?
Or does it simply provide the killers another
    fresh-poured concrete platform
        from which to throw their knives?

———

In his newspaper, *Attack,* 1928, Goebbels wrote: "We go into the
Reichstag in order to acquire the weapons of democracy from its
arsenal. We come as enemies! Like the wolf tearing into the flock
of sheep, that is how we come."

Was it possible to realize at the time
    what a tragic forewarning
        this would become?
How does one rebut the oft-repeated error
    that Hitler was democratically elected
        to dictatorship
without tearfully remembering
    Article 48
        of the Wiemar Constitution?
Or how a mass grave could be called "Operation
    Harvest Festival," a lofty Orwellian label
        designed to produce consent
so many who read the papers
    and many who pulled the triggers
        could continue to deny & deny
even as they looked
    each other
        indirectly in the eye?
Who that remembers Walter Darre as inventor
    of phrase "blood and soil" will say fascism
        sprang from too much reason?

———

Let's not forget to praise resisters—Julius Leber traveling
    the country to thread a more tightknit left,
        Sophie Scholl & her brother assembling youth

into a White Rose of refusal, Pastor Niemoller
    & Jesuit Alfred Delp urging clergy
        into emergency leagues,
New Beginnings, founded by SPD and KPD dissidents
      pushing the Popular Front, Red Orchestra's
          outspoken intellectuals, Warsaw Ghetto uprisers
Wallenberg deflecting death for thousands,
    rebels & rescuers, known & unknown,
        the brave who succeeded,
and the countless who failed.

———

What does remembering names and dates
    have to do with the feel
        or burning of human flesh?
Fill in these blanks, dear reader:
January 30, 1933 Hitler is made _____
_____, the Reichstag fire decree gives Hitler
    national emergency powers
March 23, 1933 the _____ Act abolishes the Reichstag
April 17, _____ the first anti-semitic law removes Jews
    from civil service posts
May 2, 1933, SA and __ take over labor union offices
The book _____ occur May 10, 1933
July __, 1933, German one-party state proclaimed on
    anniversary of French storming the Bastille
June 30, 1934 final consolidation of _____.

—

8

—So, then the war started 1939.
How did you hear about the war?
— Then it already was in the papers
all over, that the war is on and Hitler
is gonna come in and take all the Jews.
Take them to work. We never thought, I mean,
the word was they were not gonna kill us,
just gonna take the Jews and take them to
work in Germany because they need
workers. And we were gonna be real well off.
But that was all lies. And then we were in
a ghetto three or four months and then they
picked us up one morning and they put us
all in these cattle cars and took us. . . .

—

9

My first Middlesex Interfaith Partners with the Homeless Out-
reach Center client was a woman with hand smashed by auto-
mated conveyor belt sent mistakenly on superhuman high speed
chase. I learned to escape Daedalian social service mazes working
immense complications of her case. I called the Welfare Board,
who referred me to Homeless Prevention, who transferred me to
Youth and Family Services who gave me a phone number discon-
nected two weeks ago. She was an assembly-line full-timer with

minimum wage and no medical insurance. Disability checks were delayed by bureaucratic error yet Eviction Brigade was charging with not a moment's hesitation. Tomorrow, she would be locked out despite a full jingling key ring. County Welfare had treated her case number as if a smashed hand the newest unidentifiable communicable plague. In my office, her two boys were loud and rowdy. When I wasn't looking, one took a dump on our waiting room carpet. The boys were unruly even in guarded government offices where weekly they watched mom carrot-and-sticked like the family child. After watching mom degraded over and under, was it social context that created such uncontrollable kids? Was it Poverty's Pressurecooker? Alienating schools? So-called religious institutions? TV daily news broadcasts showing only disconnected random violence first dozen minutes every channel on the dial? Or was it fundamentally the family's fault, inadequate weak-willed mom, tragic young father death crash, untreated disordered genes filling these kids' torn Levis? How to be sure without correcting social ills? Or do nothing but read the paper four years later about an 18-year old with familiar name shooting a college student in the back ten minutes from inner city where violence thought to be contained?

—⚿—

10

—Could you tell who were the ss and who
were Hungarians?
—Sure, the ss men were in uniforms.
They had these, uh, swastikas, on their clothes,

and the Hungarians were not the soldiers
or police—just regular people.
—But the Hungarian police were not
resisting? They were helping?
—They were cooperating, cooperating.
They were helping the Germans to get us
faster out.
—So then your whole family was put on
one train car?
—Yes, we were all together in one wagon,
in one train. But not just one family:
They pushed us all in there. But one day they
said: Okay, now we're gonna take you all.
And it was before Passover. My poor
mother got together the Passover
dishes for taking into the ghetto
because Passover's coming. That was like
April. Then, they didn't let us have dishes.
They let us have whatever clothes we had—
to put everything on—so we took nightgowns,
dresses. They didn't let us have any packages,
just like one suitcase, and we took that suitcase
with us and we went. And that train stopped
in Auschwitz. Everything was lighted up.
But we didn't see any people around,
just wires. The whole thing was wired around
and we saw these chimneys—that was the
crematorium. And the light was on.
We didn't know what the hell was going on
and when we came off the trains then the ss

men were there. They put the men and the boys
on one side and the women and children,
the girls, on another side. And my mother
had three little girls, the babies, so I
went there to help her pick up the little
girl—helping with my sister. The ss men
took away my sister, dropped her to
my mother. And they took my two other
sisters and myself in one spot, because
we were older so we can go to work.
And the other kids went on the one side
and they went all right away in the
crematorium.

—⚷—

11

The shape
of the world

changes

too rapidly
for new

graphite globes
to keep up.

Old globes
break

into odd-shaped
stenotopic fragments

swept under
digitally designed

empyreal/imperial
handmade rugs

of modern art
museums

where gleaming
nonetheless

they fetch millions

from investors
in contemporary antiques

while those bound
by land

and clocks
try our best

with 3-D glasses
to read the shape

of unpredictable maps
to follow.

12

—And you saw them walking away?
—Yeah, just walking a little bit, like to
here from across the street.
—That was the last time you saw . . . ?
—That's the last I saw my parents, yes, my
mother and father.
—I remember once you told me that there
was an older woman when you were coming
into Auschwitz who saw the smoke in the
chimneys and said that's the crematorium
and no one believed her.
—Well, they took us in that night. They gave us
a bath, gave us showers, and my sister
Ann they took away separate to give
her a shower. And then Marcy and I
stayed for the next group to go under the
shower. Then I see my sister in
another group, all shaved up and naked.
So I said to Marcy, look they put us
with the crazy people. Because, in Europe,
the crazy people they shaved. They had no
hair. And then I went a little closer
and that was Ann, my sister. Then they put
us there. They shaved us. They took all the
clothes away, shoes, everything. And coats.
In April it was still cold. And they only
gave us a striped dress; that's all we had.

No underwear, no nothing. And then we
were sitting in that group all together.
A thousand girls shaved and it was cold and then
the ss men—were ladies ss, too,
and men—then the ladies came and did something,
like with a sponge, and sponged us here and there
and all over where hair was, we shouldn't get lice.
But it was very painful, it was like . . .
I don't know . . . burned. It burned like. And then we
waited. Then they gave us wooden shoes, no
stockings, no nothing, and put us up in
a camp. No, not a camp, in a barn, where
the cows lived. They took out the cows and we
went into a barn. And then a thousand
people lived in one barn. And then they had
like this room each one, and six of us got
one blanket. So we had to sleep on top
of each other with one blanket. We were
freezing and crying, but we couldn't do
nothing.
—And this was your first night?
—First night.

13

what does it mean to work for justice in your home country
as the planet becomes one huge imf cd rom gatt internet?
what's a nation in a world where electroshock treatments

cross borders with unstoppable ease? when even the moon's shadow holds within it crack epidemics and centuries of ethnic conflict? when back on the sun, it's haymarket square year-round and hangings haunt every uranium street corner? when extinct lions roar through evolutionary cyberspace dreams and revolutionary facial creams? when incurable immune viruses swim neglected mercury rivers and scapegoats are once more cheaper than fiberglass guns or imitation butter?

by the time our packed new brunswick vans rolled into 1987 boston, i had come to believe rosa luxemburg, martin luther king and abbie hoffman could squeeze behind the wheel of doctor williams's car. rutgers students were organizing a countrywide convention of student activists & i went, with my now ex-partner, to the first planning meeting as a thirty-year-old supportive observer. it was a wild & wooly intellectual affair. the rutgers contingent, mostly democratic left, proposed accountable structures. new england students, more anarchistic, argued any national structure would be a priori oppressive—they favored regional organizing, consensus decisions, no leaders accountable or not. i wondered why take on a nectarous national project if against it from initial swig. why limit to region when dominant powers reaching for more international strangleholds? won't unaccountable elites be born if no accountable ones elected? at one point, rutgers's most well-read student remarked in frustration: i can't believe you're making the same foolish mistake foucault made in '68. you say that bourgeois justice is not justice at all. but justice is justice. we need to expand it. that sounded pretty good to me, but i hadn't read foucault yet. the 40 resplendent hearts here gave me hope for america's next. but the right had money to measure & bind. the left: differing values & discourses to debate & decipher. america's rightward

march could only be halted by more unity than seemed likely any-
time soon.

        beginning 1989, gusts of change toppled the east bloc's
most intractable pillars. then mandela's prison door blew unex-
pectedly open. maybe change will spring sudden here, too, per-
haps national public policy gripping down to prepare for
awakening. for the moment, u.s. seems a sisyphean mass hooked
to cold war's ironclad anchor even while elevated experts pro-
nounce done-deal victory. meaningful social change won't be easy.
it'll take democratic experiment. not a cult of the new, but perhaps
a new third party. maybe the new party or campaign for a new
tomorrow or 21st century party or labor party advocates or the
greens or the blue horse cafe, one awe-inspiring day we'll see
where coalitional momentum develops.

        one can repair the cosmos
by anything one does, even listening to the breath of the atmos-
phere unwinding. but in politics, as abbie used to say, it's never
enough merely to be on the side of the angels.

— ⚷ —

14

—And by the first night, it was just you and
your two sisters?
—Yes, my mother and father were gone.
Then the next morning when we got up . . .
—This was still April?

—It was April, before Passover. Maybe
it was already Passover. But then
when we woke up, then each barrack—about
a thousand people was a barrack—each
had two ladies over us, Polish ladies.
Because they were there already so many
years. Two ladies had to take care of us
and then when we got up in the morning
we asked: "Where are my parents? Where can we
meet them?" And then the chimney was the flame
going out, and they said, "They're in Himinlaga."
"What do you mean Himinlaga?" That means
they're in Heaven. And there they're burning.
That's what they, she, told us. They were very
angry at us.
—I think you first told me that people didn't
believe her when she said that.
—No, nobody believed it. We thought she
was so mean. Because she was mean to us.
She was very angry at us. How could
intelligent people figuring without
a fight to come here? Why didn't you struggle . . . ,
put up a fight and don't come here? We just,
we just went literally like lambs. Because
we were promised to go to work. And we
never went to work. As we went in the
wagon—my father was in World War I.
He recognized the mountains through the little
window the train has, that these mountains are
Polish mountains. We aren't going to work
this way, we're going to Poland.

—So you thought you were going to Germany?
—We thought we were going to Germany
to work, and meantime we went to Poland.
Auschwitz was Poland.
—Had you heard of Auschwitz before?
—Never. No, no, nobody heard of Auschwitz.
We couldn't *believe* it. Who would believe *that?*

15

With hundreds of countries, thousands of cities, millions of communities,
    and billions of people on this beautiful blue planet,
how do three major TV stations end up showing the same news items
    night after endless random bullet night?
Is that why they call those faces turning serious for the camera "anchorpersons"?
Along the *Nightline* news van's bumpy ride where genocides and nonevents
    battle for their labels—
Inside GE/NBC executive suites where new ways to neglect nuclear cleanup are daily
    devised—
Amid Republican congress's stealthy new chambers where gold-throned welfare
    collectors wandering lazy streets with metal detectors, undocumented outer
    space workers clogging the city's hospital corridors, affirmative action
    magazines playing on too many virtual reality screens, sharp-toothed
    feminist shadows dimming Super Bowl 38's quarterback battles, happy
    couples with two moms building purple army-morale bombs, and Karl
    Marx's nationally endowed & endeared museum-exhibited expressionist
    beard all vie for Scapegoat Mythic Model of the Year;
where today's youth find a sexy safe peace-dividend place to celebrate
    their bright future proclaimed by smiling punditry at Cold War's end?

16

—How long were you and your two sisters at
Auschwitz?
—When we got to Auschwitz, we were there six
months. There, there was no work. Every day
we had to get up in the morning, staying
in line. And when we got very skinny—
we had no food. We got skinny, and they
always picked out the skinny people to
go to the crematorium. We went
once a week—once a day—we had to bring
in food with some big cans to feed the girls.
And bringing from the kitchen to our barrack
was like a half an hour walk. When they
gave us underwear, we took potato
peelings and we hid them, hiding them in
our underpants. And then we washed them and
that's what we cooked. And that's why we were a
little bit stronger than other people.
—What kind of food did they give you each day?
—Each day they gave us, let's say, a can from
here to the floor, a big can.
—So that's about a 2-foot can?
—Yes, and there they gave us soup, potatoes,
sometimes a little meat. Not many times.
—So they gave you a 2-foot can with soup
and potatoes for how many people?

—Well, not just one, but we had to go and
bring it in for all the thousand girls.
Quite a few people had to carry this.
But the weak kids couldn't carry that so
we had to volunteer, the strongest ones,
to carry that from the kitchen to the
barrack and then they gave us a little dish.
We had to keep our own dish, and they gave
us a little soup. One bowl of soup a day.
Just one soup a day. And then they gave us
like a loaf of bread cut into four pieces.
And each girl got one quarter of a piece
of bread a day.

—⚷—

17

When American bombs tornadoed Iraq the day after MLK's birth-
day, a hundred of us met at New Brunswick's YWCA to mourn, plan
protests, and watch large-screen TV as Bush's latest Orwellian
speech invoked Tom Paine to justify homicidal adventurism. While
Pentagon spokesmen tried on more alibis than striped neckties,
the nation's hawks knew in their fanged hearts this attack was
motivated by oil profits and military macho. After all, this the
same Saddam, Sodom, or Say-damn—pronunciation by politi-
cians and press dependent on party affiliation and whether war had
already begun—that Bush & Bergen-Belsen-ss-grave-wreath-lay-
ing Ronald Reagan funded years despite a clearly traceable trail of
monstrous poison gas footprints.

Iraq was viciously criminal to invade Kuwait, but I supported longer U.N. sanctions and talks, not short spin-cycle bombing of thousands in the name of defending ethically dry desert monarchs of Saudi Arabia and Kuwait. King George would have rolled over in his overthrown grave watching 20th-century American military camouflage protecting Saudi's public guillotine feats and royal misogynist streets where women not even allowed to drive a car. With numerous bombing "sorties" reported, it was evident to all at the Y that thousands of Iraqi civilians and young draftees were getting killed, but all one could find on any TV channel was mechanical technobabble about college-educated bombs and a few tearless trails of "collateral damage." Cable TV had added dozens of stations to the digital dial, but not one mixed humane ingredients into First Night's recipe. Computerized maps showed take-off routes and planned paths of ABD bombs that generals assured us were about to pass their doctoral exams. Not one picture of a body at eternal rest, as if newest television technology had developed war photo filters to keep out the uninvited dead. Once the bombs flew, almost no news reports noticed ten thousand grassroots USA groups just saying no to this war. Both politicians and press had learned Vietnam's lessons very well and all wrong.

At antiwar meetings, we brainstormed plans for sanity-enhancing acts. Agreement against war was clear, but so were differences about tactics, strategies, U.N. sanctions, and whether Saddam was a mass murderer or a misunderstood freedom fighter standing tough against U.S. imperialism, a poor kitty defense I didn't understand. We decided to put the ought-to-be-easy questions aside for the night and start a peaceful march down Hub City's George Street. Unlike prewar marches, this time the local press didn't show. With war on, public tolerance was shrinking fast. Half the polled prewar public opposed war, but tonight yellow ribbons were flying all over town. Many on the sidelines had cheered our earlier marches. Hecklers had kept their distance. Now, even the cars grew mean. One Cadillac at my back gave my heel an antithetical whack. Right then I knew my earlier public prophecy of mass rallies if bombs dropped would prove my poorest political prediction yet. Other marchers were stunned by cars traveling even greater velocities. This was going to be a tough war to stop. We didn't know how long it would last. Pentagon propaganda had exaggerated Iraq's Republican Guard to epic proportions to conjure illusion of a fair fight. Threats of Iraq using chemical & biological weapons were hurled. 690,000 young Americans were coerced to take experimental vaccines & pills in amnesiac violation of Nuremburg's bills. This would be a war without a neat ending. That prediction remains.

After it became clear Iraq's army held no magic hammers, Saddam offered a preground war proposition— to withdraw from Kuwait on promise of future Mideast peace talks—that was bushwhacked. The world's most expensive tanks then drove over breathing draftees. Some of Uncle Sam's smartest bombs forgot to hand in their homework. Like a good company doctor, the press kept the goriest details strictly confidential. Patriotic antimissile missiles created unfriendly fire that few had inclination to describe. The body bags that did return snuck around concerto press conferences. Iraqi death counts were painted with neo-abstract brush strokes. Bush's popularity soared and even Democrats volunteered standing ovations.

After war's end, Saddam's Mideast peace talks were held without him. Gulf War

Syndrome, with muscle weakness, sores, fevers, hair loss, joint immobility, burning genitals, and odd cancers may be caused by the vaccines, chemical or biological weapons, uranium-tipped missiles, even oil well fires, who the hell knows? U.S.Gulf War casualty figures thus remain open-ended, while military manufacturers can once again afford to send their kids to private schools.

—⚷—

18

—And were you asked to do work? You said that
you were good at sewing.
—No, no, no, we never did anything.
We were sitting there waiting to die or
take us to work. Because every day
there were people going out.
—In *Schindler's List,* there were a lot of lines.
Were they taking people out into lines
and looking people over each day?
—Yes, every day, yes.
—I remember you once telling me that
Dr. Mengele used to be there sometimes.
—Right. We had to go out six o'clock in
the morning, staying naked in the line.
He came over to check who is skinny,
who is strong. And then, if he saw some young,
good-looking girls, blond hair and nice hands, he
took them out. Then he gave us this tattoo.

Everybody wanted to have the
tattoo, the number, because whoever
got a number was hoping to go to
work one day. But we were too skinny. He
never wanted to give us a number
to go to work. And then he took them out
at night, these beautiful girls, and put them
in one barrack, separating sisters
from mothers. And they, poor girls, were crying.
And then he took them out to the soldiers,
to the front, the good-looking girls, and he gave
them nightgowns. One girl, we found out afterwards,
she wrote a note and left these notes in the
barracks. She was the oldest person there.
A Polish man who knew what these ss men
were doing when they put them separate,
the beautiful girls, saw what was going on.
He managed to bring in poison for these
kids, for these beautiful girls. And this one
person gave all the kids, told them what's gonna
happen, and gave them all poison before
the Germans came—to take this poison. They
took it and they all died. So in the morning
when he came to pick up these girls they were
all dead.
—How many were there?
—Hundreds, hundreds. And then in the morning,
we found out they were all dead. And then we
saw we had to take out the bodies in

a group where the apple, or I don't know,
who the hell. . . .
—Did you put them in a pile?
—In a pile.

19

—Dad, can you tell me about your life
during the Depression?
—When I was younger, I never knew we
were in the Depression. I knew we didn't
have a lot of money, but we didn't
know any difference. I knew it was
a major problem one day when I was
probably about 10 or 12 years old,
and my younger brother was playing with
a half dollar that my parents had left
on the table. And he dropped it between
some cracks in the wall. It was a major
thing that we should find it. I remember
that vivid incident so I assume
we were quite poor because a half dollar
was so important to my parents that
they got excited about losing it.
—Do you remember whether your father
liked the New Deal or Franklin Roosevelt?
—He was not strong on politics. Politics
was something that was in the background and
not something in the forefront.

—Was that true about you as well?

—It was true about me as well. I had
no appreciation for politics—
right, left, middle. At that time, we were too
busy earning a living, and worrying
about food on the table. And I was
worried about school.

—Where did you get your compassionate
temperament from?

—I think part of it is attitude. My
parents were open-minded toward
people and did not have any major
prejudices. They treated everyone
like they would want to be treated themselves.
And I did a lot of reading even
in high school.

—Once the war began, families could not
easily escape world affairs. You joined
the army, right?

—I volunteered for the army in
'43. And went in, actually,
after two years of college. I served three
years. I did basic training at Edgewood
and went overseas from Oakland,
California, on a boat that zigzagged
over the Pacific Ocean until
we got to New Guinea. I was in New
Guinea maybe about three or six months.
And then went on what was called, I believe,
an LST boat—a boat with a

very flat bottom, such that when we went
from New Guinea to the Philippines the
boat would rise up and slap the water
until it looked like it would fall apart.
As we were traveling, you could see welders
on other boats in the convoy. And it
was not a comfortable feeling. I'm
not enthused about cruises or going
on the water since then—I'm allergic
to going on water. I was in the
Philippines, Manila, on vj Day,
when victory over Japan was called.
I was one of the first troops that went
into Japan to take control of many
Japanese weapons that were handed to
u.s. troops.
—Were you wounded at one time?
—I wasn't wounded. While I was in Japan,
it was found that I had a spinal cyst.
I had an operation in the u.s.
Army's Tokyo area. I came
home on a hospital ship—Japan to
San Francisco. They operated on
my back in Japan. I was on my stomach
three weeks while the wound was healing. So I
was in pretty bad shape on my back quite
awhile. It may have been related to
an infection in New Guinea, but it
was not a war wound. I was never
really on the front lines of the action.

I was on secondary lines, although
a good friend got a secondary
assignment with an Air Force group near us
and he was killed in a crash.
—What made you volunteer? Did you know what
was at stake? Did you know the Nazis were
exterminating Jews?
—I knew that the Nazis were antagonistic
to Jews. I didn't really know that they
were exterminating Jews. I don't think
that was really too well known. I knew, though,
that they were punishing Jews and not treating
them well. And then I was disturbed by the
Japanese attack at Pearl Harbor. I
had a patriotic feeling about
our country. I knew that our country had
been doing some good.
—When did you find out the extent of the
genocide against European Jews?
—I never really knew the extent of
genocide until, I think, well after
I was back in the United States after
the war was over. I didn't realize
the extent until after I met your
mother. When she emphasized the tales of
horror, then I really could see the factors
involved in Hitler's holocaust.
—Tell me what it was like to be with someone
who had just gone through such horrible
tragedy.

—I could tell that she must have had a very
traumatic experience because she
was very nervous. You could see how she
reacted to sudden noises with shock.
Walking on the street with her, if a
policeman went by, you could see a
traumatic reaction. Often, when I
was sleeping with her, she would wake up
screaming, shivering, or sweating. That was
the case during the early years of marriage.
So you could see they went through very
difficult times. They were still not recovered.
I tried to support her and gradually,
I think, up to the present time, those fears
have eased.

20

—I know there must have been incredible
sadness about your family. And fear
about what was going to happen to
you and your two sisters. Can you talk about
some of the mental survival strategies
that you used to get to the next day?
—Yes, because we never believed our parents
are dead. We thought this lady's so mean,
she tells us that they're in Himinlaga.
We never believed it. To the bitter end,

we didn't believe that people could do
so much to other people. And we didn't
believe that they killed them.
—Until when?
—Probably until we were liberated.
—Even after you went to two other
camps, you still thought at the end of the war
you would see your family again?
—That's right, that's right, that's right. Because after
the war when we were liberated we
wanted to go home to Hungary to find
our parents. We couldn't believe it. Yet,
we were in such a condition there, that
they died every morning—and burying—
when we were first in Auschwitz. Then finally
they took people out to work. When they came
into our barrack, they needed more people
to do work, so they took my two sisters
in the line. And me, they wouldn't take
because I was very skinny already.
So I was hiding in the barrack where
I wouldn't go into that line where they
go to Auschwitz—I mean to the
crematorium—because I didn't
want to be with the skinnier people.
So I ran to the toilet and there came
a little girl, about 10 or 12 years old.
She spoke very beautiful German so
they liked this kid. She was in her regular
clothing, civilian clothes, dressed elegant.

She used to help count—a messenger she
was. She came into the barrack, into
the toilet, and said: Why are you crying?
I said there are my two sisters in that
line and I can't go there because they
separated me. And I wanna go there.
So she took off her jacket. She says: Okay,
take my jacket, put it on, and you go
to the line. And when you get to the line,
drop my jacket off and I'll go pick it up.
So I did that. Then, when they had to count
a thousand people, the last line was one
more person. So there was a young kid with
a mother. They separated the mother.
They threw away the mother and the kid
came with us. And I felt all my life so
guilty. She was an elderly person
and might not have survived. But that's when
I took away somebody else's spot.
—I showed you earlier this book, *Holocaust
Testimonies*. And it seems like almost
everyone who survived the death camps
has a story like that. It was so random.
The violence was so random.
—Right, yes, right. . . .

— 21

Dadaism   Imagism   Surrealism

Objectivism   Vorticism   Futurism

Expressionism   Dynamism   (Auschwitz-Birkenau)

— 22

—How did you go on? Did you have hope?
Were you thinking about what you would do
when you got out?
—Yes, I always had hope that I'll survive.
Somehow, somewhere, God is gonna let me
live. Because we were religious people,
brought up religious by my father. We
always prayed that we should survive. In fact,
that was my pledge: If I ever survive,
I always will help other people.
—So, you were actually thinking that
at the time?
—Yes, always.
—And you were praying?
—I was praying.
—And in your prayers you were saying?
—And I said, if God lets me live, I'll always,

for the rest of my life, I'll devote to
help other people. In the back of my mind,
that's what I always thought. And I always
remembered that, and always tried to do that.
So you can see why I'm always involved,
with the phone, helping people. So, then what
happened. . . .

—○—

23

since you asked here's a national snapshot telegraph from novem-
ber 1994 step by the time you open this album things will have
moved in one direction or another step in national elections the
so-called republicans just took control of both congressional
homes step a pesty newt has nipped the clintons' neck calling the
couple countercultural mcgoverniks step ah if only if only if only
step the cold war must be reinvented and once firmly in place re re
re invented step ha ha ha ha ha honk step with the donkey wear-
ing elephant snout people voted the real elephant step honk honk
honk step with no progressive answer easily attainable people
often go atavistic & ballistic rather than stay the sickly status quo'
step will pendulum swing back when newest righter-wing solu-
tions prove old solutions prove no solutions or do we keep moving
even further right step step step don't wait for the red light step
step step move aside step step step outadawaylosers stepstepstep
newsflash pure american products go crazy stepstepstep make way
for the gingrich about to steal your christmas bonus and health
care package while winking for your trust with lines from your

favorite steamy drugstore novel stepstepstep let's have a warm welcome for the distinguished sepulchral senator from north carolina step he has lost his appestat and just threatened to have the president . . . step tomorrow he will be appointed the senate foreign relations chair stepstepstep stepstepstep will democrats learn some real lessons and invent a new melodic nonatomic lipotropic liberalism or will they too persist walking further to the unrequited right stepstepstep who wants to help build a new new left stepstepstop

—○⌓—

2 4

—So you had hopes that you would . . .
—Survive, yes, I always prayed I would survive.
—But were you depressed a lot? Were you
afraid also?
—Oh, sure, we always were afraid. And poor
Anna, she was once caught, they beat her up
real bad. She was caught because she went at
night to steal potatoes for us and they
caught her. And then I come in from the kitchen,
and there she is. They beat her up. They had
to give her over the naked tuchis
with the rubber thing, twenty. Everybody
was hollering. I didn't know my sister
was in there. And she never cried. She never
cried. And the ss man liked her because
she didn't cry and he stopped at ten. He

didn't beat her all the way. He stopped at ten.
Because she was always good looking, broad
shoulders. Another Jewish girl, this Polish
lady, squealed that she was stealing.
—She squealed to get in favor with the guards?
—Yeah, but those guards who were with us didn't
appreciate that. They didn't want to do it.
But if the Jewish girls themselves squeal, what
can they do? But then he felt so bad
the next day. The next day they put me in
the kitchen to cook, this ss man, because
he knew I'm Anna's sister. The Polish
lady came to say, don't take this girl because
she's Anna's sister, she'll do the same thing.
Then the ss man said to me, in German,
you're not her sister, right? He went like that
I should say no. I said no. She says, yes
she is. And the ss man went like that.
—So there were some guards who did some little
things to help . . .
—Who had a heart, yes. But these, these were not
ss men. This guy was Wermacht. They were
regular soldiers.
—Did you ever meet anybody after
the war who had any news about your
family? Who went in the line with them?
—No, nobody in the line was alive.
I don't think anybody stayed alive
after that line.

25

In the midst of early American modernism,
    35,000 workers were killed
    & over 700,000 injured
    in 1914's industrial accidents.
That year, more than 100 socialists
    elected local office
    by pure products
    of Oklahoma.
The *Brooklyn Eagle* fired Helen Keller
    after she self-declared socialist
    pointing out
    her physical limitations
as if deafness & blindness
    entered her life
    as bodily defense against
    ideological transformation.
In 1919, Seattle workers sustained a citywide strike
    nonviolently,
    about which
    Anise wrote in labor's paper:
"The businessmen / Don't understand
    That sort of weapon . . .
    It is your SMILE
    That is upsetting
Their reliance / On Artillery, brother!"
    Not many read Anise's poems anymore.
    And Seattle now renowned
    for grunge rock & coffee shops.

In 1924, KKK Nights of Abhorrent Cloth
    masked America
    with over 4.5 million
    white hoods.
In 1932, the Bonus Army came to DC
    imploring early depression-era payment
    of World War I bonuses
    already pledged:
twenty thousand vets were smacked back
    by MacArthur, Eisenhower, & Patton—the best
    military minds the U.S.
    could muster against its own.
Opposing the most elegant thuggery
    big business could buy,
    1.5 million U.S. unionists nonetheless
    went on strike 1934.
Since then wars have been fought—
    wars have been stopped.
    MLK's birthday declared a holiday—
    his radical democratic legacy quietly ignored.
Developing World materials and misery
    prop up the western wardrobe
    yet laughter & music become
    more internationalized than ever.
Despair / Desire, sorrow / hope, stenotopic /
    eurytopic—old stories witnessed
    in new ways. What is history
    if not a bit of wishful thinking?

26

—So, how did you end up leaving Auschwitz?
You were there for one year?
—No. Six months we were in Auschwitz. Then they
took us to work in Ober Schlesien, where
the movie *Schindler's List* was made. We were
in that town, but not in his camp.
—What was that called?
—Oberschlasser's in Krakow, Krakow.
—So you were in Krakow?
—Yes, Krakow. But not in his camp. We had
another camp where we were in the outskirts
digging schaufelngrab, digging ditches, for
the soldiers to hide. When the war came closer,
they hid in those ditches. We made the ditches.
We were in the same town, but we didn't know
each other. I wish I would have been in
his camp.
—You and your two sisters were still together?
—Right. We werc always together.
—And how were the conditions in Krakow?
Were they the same as in Auschwitz?
—No, no, no, no. In Krakow, was a little
bit better because we were working.
Every morning we went to work. Then
at night we had hay still in the cows' barracks.

The cows they took out, but they left the hay
so we slept on the hay. But each person
got a blanket. We got clothes back. We got
underwear. We got a sweater. And that
is when we got our own clothes back. Then we
started looking in the envelope, in
the shoulder pads, and we opened them up
and I found 20 dollars. And when I
found the 20 dollars I gave it to
this German guy who was in the kitchen.
I said I got 20 dollars, please tell
them I should work here with you peeling
potatoes. And I said—he was so dumb—
I said this 20 dollars can buy you
a whole house and he believed me. And he
took my 20 dollars and didn't squeal
on me. He could have squealed. And he put me
into the kitchen to peel potatoes.
That's why I had it pretty good. I never
went out to the ditches.
—Did they feed you better in Krakow than
they did in Auschwitz?
—Yes, we had all the foods. I cooked the food.
And we had cow's meat.
—And you weren't as worried about getting
sent to the crematorium?
—No. Not there, there was no crematorium.
—So once you were in Krakow it seemed like
you were going to survive?
—Yes.

—And was the ss still there?

—Yes.

—Did Mengele visit this camp?

—No, Mengele was gone. Mengele stayed
in Auschwitz. He never came with us.
But then Auschwitz was evacuated
because the Russians came. As we ran, we
saw the bombing, the fire. And then even
the ss men, the Wermacht—it wasn't
the ss men—said don't come with us, please
don't come, stay here. Hide in the woods. Run away.
The war is almost over. Don't come, because
you're gonna get killed. Run run. And many
of our kids ran. Ran away to deep in
the woods. And they stayed alive. And I was
afraid to run. Anna wanted to run.
I said no, let's stay together. Because
sometimes when we ran away they were shooting
us. We couldn't believe them. Are they gonna
shoot us or what?

—⚷—

27

    For first trip to self-described socialist country, I would've preferred Sandinista
Nicaragua—where democratic credentials proven by stepping off stage at elected time.
    In 1989, I took Aeroflot flight Pyonyang, North Korea—part of diverse 100-
person u.s. delegation to 13th World Festival of Youth & Students.

Every North Korean citizen wore lapel button with Great Leader's snap-shot—every third billboard marked days Great Leader had stood that spot—museums exhibited pot from which Great Leader scooped boiled potatoes—

he alone defeated Japanese & Americans—built world's first electric tractor—personally taught each farmer to plant rice—he who built world's tallest hospital—Pyonyang's material development did seem impressive & well distributed.

But officials removed all banners honoring slain student Tianenmen heroes, nonevent in North Korea's state-run press—no disabled persons visible anywhere—lesbians from Denmark forced to add second clubhouse balloon "except in Korea" to original "lesbians are everywhere"—

I wandered into private meeting North Korea's Ministry of Culture—amiably asked about my poems—to inquire any curiosities—"don't hold back"—

I wanted be polite—ease future friendship possibilities—was thankful for generosity of guides and astounding friendliness felt on sidewalk—also nervous in secluded smoke-filled back room—

asked who owned printing presses—"the state"—I described subtle and overt market limits on American literary publishing—asked criteria here—"high aesthetic quality" and "educating the people"—15 novels 600 short stories and over 1,000 poems printed each year—Kim Il Sung over 1,000 lifetime books—does tradition of love poems exist?—"yes, love for the people"—said I thought people might like to hear some private love poems too—

We'd come for festival and weren't disappointed—huge international panels with u.n.-style translation headphones held in six centers—

first night, danced Nicaragua's clubhouse, Hasenfus's captured CIA parachute and made-in-USA plastic C4 explosives displayed on wall—

u.s. delegates met daily with youth I might never visit: Salvador, Sweden, Soviet Union, Yugoslavia, Vietnam, African National Congress, Sinn Fein,

Israeli & PLO Peace Movements—who could foresee how quickly
Soviet Union cease to exist?—Yugoslavia devolve decompressed
ethnocentric civil warred slaughters?—

how soon ANC take its longshot presidential seat?—strides
taken toward pacifistic two-state Mideast cessation to bulldozing
rifle occupations and terrorist detonations?—

Older members chaired meetings—my turn with Vietnamese—
soulful privilege for one so shaped by reading antiwar
movement—which I described—offered hopes for renewed
relations & presented gift Abbie Hoffman memorial T-shirt—

they didn't know Abbie but apprehended gesture—knew
American youth, even soldiers, had not been military decision-
makers—their expressed historical forgiveness a bit surreal—

most had lost family, friends—some walked artificial plastic
legs, shook hands with one arm left—after 7 million bomb tons
& 3 million deaths, now offering total friendship—economically
imperiled, even inviting U.S. to dig into oily shores—proposed
official trade accord shaped right there—had brought along TV
cameras & binding signatories—

as contingent's chair, perhaps I should've signed?—but
explained in diplomatic cadence we were basically ragtag group
concerned youth with wide spectrum political ideas but no official
backing—our signatures would not adhere—I could autograph
the T-shirt but a treaty light-years beyond my humble grasp—

Vietnamese delegates laughed—then we had a party—amazing
how young people could get along without official obstacles
in the way.

—So you were older than your sisters and
you were making a lot of the decisions?
—Yes, and they listened to me, my two sisters.
—That was a heavy responsibility
for somebody who was still in their teens.
—We had to, because we saw how they killed them.
From Auschwitz, we went to Bergen-Belsen
first before we went to other places.
—Before Krakow?
—No. After Krakow. When the war came closer
there, everybody ran and we ran
and we ran. Finally, in the morning,
they took us again to another place.
But we had to walk. The train was no train,
because they were bombing. So we had to
walk for six weeks. To Bergen-Belsen.
—So you were in Auschwitz for six months?
—Yes.
—Then how long were you in Krakow for?
—About three months.
—For three months. And then you began to walk
for six weeks?
—To Bergen-Belsen. We were there six weeks.
We were liberated in Bergen-Belsen.

29

Thomas Paine: "The vanity and presumption of governing
beyond the grave is the most ridiculous and insolent
of all tyrannies. . . . It is the living and not the dead
that are to be accommodated."

Paine's uncommon legacy: To see with interpretive eyes
beyond the Founding Fathers' original intentions—
and yet, what to do with all those buried allies
that long to be embraced?

Despite some disproportionately long claws, history is not only
a memoir of superpowers. Look at Khmer Rouge murders,
Mobutu's pillage, Baltic & Rwandan ethnic conflict
reborn in modern genocide's nest.

It's difficult to be certain where imperialism's malinfluence ends,
but it's clear India's slaughters outlasted British rule.
In Mideast, the proof is plain to read
in Torah, Koran, New Testament:

So why hasn't the god of oil & water crowned its victor yet?
U.S. role in Latin American death squad force is undeniable,
yet those countries have their own home-grown hit men
of horror who ought not to be forgot.

But all nations have purple ribbons of heroic democracy as well:
a nation like an artistic form never embodying
    mere monolithic potential—a toast offered here
    to a dazzling array of American traditions:

To Tom Paine, Harriet Tubman, W.E.B. Du Bois, Emma Goldman,
Ella Baker, Norman Thomas, Charlotte P. Gilman, César Chávez,
    MLK, Abbie, Mother Jones, Izzy Stone,
    Sitting Bull, Joe Hill, C. Wright Mills,

League of the Iroquois, Seneca Falls Declaration of Sentiments,
Port Huron Statement, Harrington's Other America, the Nearings'
    Good Green Life—too many to name, so stop now,
    to be continued another day—

a toast to Gandhi's earth-shaking marches
& to Rosa Luxemburg who insisted a new society
    could never be built by decree, who wrote:
    "freedom is always and exclusively freedom

for the one who thinks differently," who predicted:
"Without general elections, without unrestricted freedom
    of press and assembly, without a free struggle
    of opinion, life dies out in every public institution,

becomes a mere semblance of life, in which only
the bureaucracy remains"—to dissident poets dead or alive
    who have raised the ceiling of human potential:
    Akhmatova, Claribel Alegría, p'Bitek, Brecht, Hikmet,

Blake, Breton, Serge, Szymborska, Cesaire,
Cardnal, Cavafy, Neruda, Mayakovsky,
    Whitman, Doolittle, Rukeyser, Hughes,
    Ginsberg, Baraka, Reznikoff, Rich—

millions of visions known & unknown from which to draw—
how much did America's most well-known modernist poets
    know of popular democracy, accountable institutions,
    all citizens with a say in the social & economic decisions

affecting their lives?— brilliant elegant Ezra making a pact
to begin with Whitman, then chipping away
    the most democratic slivers—a dream
    perhaps unfinishable, but one we can aim toward,

across borders, utopian & all, even across temporary boundaries
of life and death: Illuminated Vision remains lit—though the body
    be exiled or imprisoned, struck by
    invisible sniper or unspeakable crime.

—⚷—

30

—And where did you sleep on the way? You just
slept along the road?
—On the snow, along the road, wherever
we felt we laid down on the snow since we
couldn't walk. But all these kids who couldn't walk
anymore stayed in the back. And Anna,

since she was still strong, had to dig the graves
to bury them. Because whoever couldn't
walk they just shot 'em, the ss men.
Because they couldn't walk anymore, what
can you do with them? There was no wagon
to carry them, nothing. So he shot them
and buried them there. And quite a few,
my sister buried them. Her own girlfriend
they had to kill there and bury there.
—So then you went to Bergen-Belsen?
—Then we got to Bergen-Belsen. We slept
twelve in two rooms of beds. We slept there, with
very little food. And then they gave us
some kind of poison, not poison, some kind
of medicine that we should never get
our periods. So, nobody had
periods. They put us together with
Russian people, too, not Jewish. And they
went to work every day. They couldn't treat
them like us. They were fighting. They were shooting,
fighting. I don't know how they got guns, but
they were shooting, fighting.
—The Russians in the camp with you had guns?
—In the camp. Had hidden guns. Somehow, somewhere.
I don't know how they got them. Maybe they
slept with the ss men, who the hell knows?
And they were strong. We were so weak. They were
sleeping in the daytime and going to
work at night.
—Were they helping you at all?

—No, no. They felt sorry. They had to fight
for their own lives. But they had more food and
blankets. So in the daytime while they were
sleeping, I used to go and steal their food,
their bread, and blankets.
—And were you again on lines every day?
—Yes. Then, when I stole the blankets, I stole
some knives from them. They had knives, too, I don't
know how they had knives. Then the ss men
came and they said whoever—because the war
came so close—whoever has knives, they can
come in the kitchen and peel potatoes.
Since I had a knife, I went to peel the
potatoes. But then they got very mad
and they came into our camp again saying:
Who knows how to sew? So Anna volunteered
with other kids. And they took them to sew
their dresses, civilian dresses. The wives
or the ss ladies threw away the
ss clothes—the war came so close—and put
on civilian dresses. Then, when she finished
the dresses, he came and banged on the kitchen
and said: Who sewed my wife's dresses? And my
sister again volunteered. She thought she's
gonna get something for it. He started
beating her up. And beating her up so bad,
hitting with a screwdriver in the head.
And made holes in her head. And we couldn't cry,
because if we cry he sees a sister.
We didn't cry. He put her in a barrel

and hit her with an ice . . . with a screwdriver—
and bleeding. Then he went away. He hit
so many like that, and then they run away
because the war was over. But we didn't know.
—So, the war was over at this time?
—Yes, but because we didn't know, he beat
all these kids up who'd sewed the dresses and
ran away. And then the war was over.
All of a sudden we had no ss
men with us. Then we saw other people
coming in. The English people came.

—○—

31

I summoned Rosa L. for a brief moment
        during midnight meditation and weeping:
"With death at hand, it wasn't my own life
        which flashed before my eyes
        but the upcoming terror:
Huge consuming fires rolling down European Hills
unprecedented earthquakes sucking entire cities
        down to the molten planet core
body appendages flying like cannonballs,
        stray elbows splashing
        into Old World fountains.
The tragedy was I knew it could be stopped—
        but for the angry glances
        of erstwhile friends.

One usually gets wiser after it's too late.
Enjoy life—in spite of everything.
Don't make a virtue of necessity.
Contribute. Humor yourself & others.
It's okay you're approaching forty
    without permanent accomplishment,
    without a career,
with long periods of uncertain love.
It's all right to spill coffee on your manuscript.
Forgive yourself. Take speech lessons.
    Exercise. Don't worry
    about tucking in your shirt.
Study the migration of birds.
Consider the general strike.
    Be experimental. Exhale."

32

—The British were the ones who came to liberate
the camp?
—Right, the British. And there were doctors.
Between the soldiers were doctors. And then
I ran to the doctor. He couldn't speak . . .
he was Belgian. He didn't know English
and we didn't know nothing.
—You only knew Hungarian at this time?
—Yes, and Jewish. A little bit German.
I talked a little bit German. But this guy

didn't know nothing. Then we brought my sister
to this man—because he said he's a doctor.
—Did they explain to your sister why they
were hitting her about the dresses?
—No.
—They didn't tell her that she didn't sew
the dresses right? Or . . .
—No, No, NO!

—⚷—

33

I worked for Middlesex Interfaith Partners
        with the Homeless
        eight years, helping to push
people's rights across stubborn legislative desks
        & cracked social service nets. Here's a few
        confidential voices of women passing through:

—I ended up homeless again. I had
domestic violence with my daughter's
father in 1989. Then I
had the TRAP program but the apartment
was condemned. The TRAP program—that stands for
Temporary Rental Assistance Program,
but everybody calls it by its nickname,
even the welfare workers. I ended
up back into the shelter again.
Then I got a motel through welfare, where

I stayed for 3 years. Welfare only paid
for the first year. I had to take them
to a judge to get that. At the end of
that year, the shelter had no room, no nothing.
So I paid the second two years at
the motel myself. There was no place
for my daughter to play, no kitchen,
only one double bed. And lots of times
the lock was broken. My whole check went
to the room. We lived on food stamps only.
I was with him 3 years, putting up with him
leaving, coming back, leaving, and coming back.
When he left for good on July 5th,
I made sure he got on the train with a
one-way ticket. I guess right after he
left, my daughter turned around and said that
she don't want—she told me what happened. Now,
I don't need nobody, which I'm glad of
'cause I don't have nobody. I finished
a college computer course. That's what I
was crying for. Half of it was happy tears.
—I'm 24. I have two children, a
3-year old and a 1-year old. When I
walked in the door, I was scared to death. When
I was pregnant with my first child, it seemed
like every move I'd try to make, the powers
that be, I must say, were not very
cooperative. I was living at home
with my mom. She was an alcoholic.
She still is. I was like "how can you judge

me" when you're sitting there getting sloshed
and peeing under the couch cause you think
it's the bathroom. When I was 9 years old
I had to dress her to take her to bed.
That was no responsibility for
a kid.
—Here was where I lived, right in the middle
of drugs and alcohol and fights and
violence and prostitutes and everything
else. This was my wonderful surroundings.
I lived with my mother, my 2 kids, my
boyfriend, my big sister, and my sister's
son in a 2-bedroom apartment.
I had my first kid when I was 20.
That's when the domestic violence problem
started, with the fighting, the arguing,
the beating. And my mother made me feel
like shit. When I was pregnant with my first,
she told me every damn day she was
embarrassed, nobody has to know, why
don't you get rid of it. She told me the
baby was shit. I can show the scars that
I got till I grew bigger than she was.
I was raised out here. It was dangerous,
but it taught you how to survive, how to
deal with shit. I was always like "fuck you."
Me and my best friends would hang around here
and tell off the people, especially
the ones who tried to push drugs. I never
did drugs. I seen everybody wasting

their lives, dying, getting sick, and I didn't
want that. There's nothing to do around here.
There is the bridge where I met him. Every
time I see it I want to blow it up.
When he went to jail that's when I became
homeless. I thought I met the man of my life
and it was the nightmare of my life. I thought,
I guess, that this was the man who was gonna
save me from my problems. And, oh lord, no.
The way it happened opened my eyes.

3 4

—So, a lot of times the violence that
they gave was not explained?
—No, no, NO! NO! On purpose. Because he
was so mad they had to run away.
And she sewed those dresses. Because they had
to run away they went crazy. The ss
men probably went crazy. Why would they
give a reward of beating them up?
—So how did you feel when the British came?
—Oh, we were very happy! But then they
did a very stupid thing, the British.
Very stupid. Because we were very
hungry. Well, the Germans poisoned the water,
we shouldn't be able to even drink
the water.

—Before they left?

—Before they left, ss men poisoned the
water. They poisoned the water so we
couldn't drink. But whoever drank got very
bad diarrhea. And all the sicknesses.
I had a little bit, a little water.
But that's why I went into the hospital.
The stupid thing the British did—they were
so dumb—they made these big packages of
food with delicious meat, like canned food.
I never saw canned food in my life. Chicken
and food and everything and very salty.
And we didn't eat a little bit at a time.
We just ate everything and that's why
they were killed, lots of kids.

—People were killed?

—Because they ate everything and then they
had to drink the poisoned water and that's
how they died. And we were all very sick.
That made us even worse, sicker than we were.
That's what killed lots of them.

35

in "frame," adrienne rich makes explicit point to situate her sub-
jective position, boston, 1979, standing just outside action frame
watching innocent undergraduate female lab student beaten by
police. such a compelling stylistic move, i vowed

to use the tactic in some future poem, so here i am, home in new jersey, at desk, transcribing tapes w/ inexpensive handheld battery recorder & laptop computer, flipping assorted historical books, tapping lucky imagination's daily secretions, bad back propped

against foam lumbar roll, here in state still nicknamed after now-extinct gardens, where famous contemporary fragrance now emanates midnight industrial elizabeth smokestack, where car window serves as jersey turnpike's respiratory guard of last resort,

whitman's restplace, now curled barbwire fence concrete cube jailhouse directly 'cross street from good gray poet's final home, state where first alleged "welfare reform" passed to deny increased grants to welfare mothers' newly born children,

new scapegoating sippet sweeping the newt republican nation. on plus side, first state introduce profound legislation mandating high-school holocaust classes—when bill introduced, some senators attempted amendatory inclusions, each press conferencing

a world genocidal lesson plan: contemporary bosnia, pol pot's cambodia, stalinist russia, turkish armenian slaughter, all named, all crucial instructions. yet no senator named even one genocide directly or indirectly american-induced—no germy blanket,

smoking monster slaveship, burnt atomic bomb, book of the dead's bhopal billows, vietnam's fiery children on the run, cancer's nuclear atmospheric blasts & rotting plutonium soup cans threatening a thousand generations, u.s. presidents whispering indonesia's east timorous ears, latin american death squads southern-hospitality-trained. as dad says, this country has truly done much good that needs carrying on. yet part of poet's citizenly duties also the daily reminder, democracy begins at home. the difficult historical decisions—

which suitcases to drop. paul revere riding through town sounding the alarm. you ask, what is home? after eight years as housing advocate, my reply still changes minute by minute. how many think home till exact moment tornado rips the roof off? how many homes

have served as mere launching pads to cattle cars, cotton fields, broken treaties, rickety boats navigating between lightning streak roars across oceanic hurricane floors? in *grapes of wrath,* muley proclaims to tom & preacher casey, "places where folks live is them folks,"

a humanity-defining protest shout, voiced just before joads forced to ride those damn lying roads. yet, homeless, many rode those roads with dignified humanity rubber cemented intact—what a different world that was, when being shoved off land was a shock,

when disillusionment with modern america actually surprised. what odd notion it would seem in contemporary novel that average characters believe in a right to own their own land, today, when american ceo's take salaries 150 times factory workers,

when 358 international billionaires own more wealth than 40% of the planet, when blake's most attentive readers instinctively know that plowed land forgives the plow but eventually is ceded to the plow's corporate manufacturer. so, where was i? 2 A.M. home writing this line, late 30s radical jewish atheist praising the infinite kabbalistic splendor of the universe, the spacious world constantly coming, extoling the sacred seed within, the brain's brain, we were born on this earth to learn, each honest insight invigorates the breath of creation,

so here offering up subjective contradictions, believing we need respect diverse histories yet transcend nationalisms & notions of pure identity. opposed to mystical paradox as policy solution, yet knowing public spiritual crisis real & relevant as housing food medical emergencies.

subconscious imagery has subverted too many activist meetings, where difference between family & state not yet clear to much youthful energetic ire. what happens after death still unsolved dilemma driving millions to stressful early graves. yes, e. katz, okay to rest awhile

in the unknown. no more teleologies! neither to guarantee success nor resigned to flubbed failure. the future unknowable—dependent on human actions here on. admitting defeat beforehand no help and non-sense. fuck adorno's anti-enlightenment pessimistic shit

that capital's culture industry will always co-opt our holiest visions, his turning the dialectic on its side where it can kick & scream, but no longer even potentially motor history along, his turning milk into iron prison camp bars. they're winning—

i can admit that. for the moment, able to incorporize both tangible & otherworldly dynamics, even innovative montage, manifold forms once thought untouchable hip techniques, indeterminate styles lurk- ing in incorruptible corners, waiting to pounce. as long as they win, they will co-opt old forms or new. that's why the whole shebang needs replanting, spring roots & all. as long as it means all have a say, i don't care what a third way is called—democratic socialism, radical democracy, liberty equality fraternity, feminist antiracist enlightened

mixed economic ecological cooperation, egalitarian democracy, simple freedom, compassion in action, blue horse, red green pepper— probably different names, some catchy & new, for different contexts. but let's begin working to win, nonviolently as possible.

martin luther king: a nation that continues to spend more money on defense than on programs of social uplift is approaching spiritual death. doctor, is there time?—to save the spiritbody's pulse, yes. maybe historically-contingent universal values

will satisfy the skeptical & safeguard our well of diverse earthly delights? ah mandela, in this often disheartening world—full of rising zhironovskys, karadziks, lepens, dukes—your election a stirring rebuke to political fatalism and tribute to principled prismatic persistence,

an anticipatory illumination & verification of hope. from his grave, i hear ernst bloch applaud. what can be imagined can be made real: poetry prefiguring the popular front, bringing the not-yet into the room. that's where i am. for the moment fending off destructive life patterns,

but not mistake-free. it took awhile to learn let pleasure-armor down w/o defeating dionysus in a gin mill round. now done alcohol self-defeat mechanism & enjoying occasional red wine toasts. i don't have walt whitman's ability to be everywhere at once,

but have tried to form a decent set of cosmic eyes. my dad grew up during
the depression. my mom is a holocaust survivor. i wouldn't be here if not
for uncle sam. in the next race, i'm betting Unrealized Possibilities and
Unspent Dreams. thanks. now i gotta go. driving,

with lyrical instincts & obsolete maps,
                        pulled steady through this magnetic
        & hazardous spiral of time

36

—Did you celebrate or were you too sick?
—No, there were no celebrations, no.
But what happened—they took home the Russian
people first. The Russian government came
and they went home. Because they were all strong.
There was a Jewish lady with a kid
and we told her don't go home. It's not gonna
be good in Russia. Come with us wherever
we go. I had an uncle in America.
We'll go to America. Come with us.
—You had an uncle in America?
—Yeah. But I didn't know an address.
But then I said, okay, let's go to Sweden.
I don't wanna go back. Whoever wants
to go back, they took 'em home. Whoever
wants to go to Sweden can go to Sweden.
And I decided we'll go to Sweden.

And then, soon as we arrived in Sweden
in the ship, we were happy then because
we were alive on a ship. And they gave
us such a beautiful home overlooking
the harbor. The most beautiful town. It's
called Vikengsill. To live there and feed us.
They didn't even let us make the beds.
Elegant ladies with diamonds came to
wash the floors for us, make the beds. I said:
What the hell? Where are we now? It was cold
in Sweden. Then they took everybody
into a big department store. We had
a right to take two coats, winter coats,
summer coats, nobody was in the store.
And two suitcases, big suitcases. We
had a ball there. Whoever wanted, take
whatever we wanted. We packed 'em and
then we took off. And that's what they did for us.
I'll never forget that. And then they took
us to operas once a month. They were nice
people. But they didn't know we were Jewish.
—They didn't?
—They thought we were Hungarians.
—And when they found out you were Jewish, they
treated you differently?
—Then they were a little bit different,
yes. But they treated us very nice.
Gentile people treated us. Jewish people
were afraid to come to us, they might catch
our sicknesses.

—How long were you in Sweden?
—From '45, three years.
—So you came to the United States
in 1948?
—Yes.
—And you had an uncle here?
—Yes. Oh, that was interesting. I didn't
know an address. I knew a Berkowitz.
Sam Berkowitz. Go find Sam Berkowitz,
right? So the Jewish organizations
always said: Give us addresses. I knew
he lives in New York and I knew he was
a furrier. How the heck can you find—
lots of Sam Berkowitzes.
—So they found him?
—No, another mother and daughter lived
with us and they had a brother. The mother
found her brother. And the brother said, please,
if there's other kids, give me their names and
I'll find them. And that mother's brother found
my uncle.

—⚷—

37

Now that even Gilgamesh drinks Pepsi Light, new international songs
    of desire fill the next century's dusty lungs
Global workers study the tune of holy planet shifts, a Sympathy Strike
    lyric rebounds off a satellite dish

National flags are ripped to shreds, fine psychedelic handkerchiefs to
 catch the new flu
Blake's ninth night arrives, when lions roar from deep furnaced caves
 amazed how it is we have walked through fires yet not been consumed
As the war of multiple discourses begins to replace daily terror of nuclear
 pocket swords & plutonium hair triggers
Reason passion sensation & instinct embrace, poetry's saxophone sounds
 the cosmopolitan call: universal citizenship shortly awaits all
Acrobatic voters tumble across ancient bugle boundaries to march in
 world literacy's welcoming parade
The endangered owl opens its eyes wide to guide the sundrenched
 carpenter where best to strike the nail
Insatiable whales bark to let the navigator know near which rocks the last
 ship disappeared
An honest wind warms an honest face, the old window blinds cry out to
 be replaced
A shooting star, the world's most renowned astronomer announces the
 galaxy will never be the same
A trustworthy politician, peace through peace, a concerned attentive
 public, a radio talk show designed to end bigotry
The sociology student who dreams herself president awakens in control
 of her cabinet's affairs
A cyberspace doorbell rings, a roving internet with potential companion
 in its sweet adhesive chords
MTV's Top Forty songs convince the world's most stubborn rock to pour
 its cool liquid forth
Divine genitals perpetually replenished, the Milky Way's dynamic power
 restored, desire below completes the symmetry above
Supersonic transport jets gravel-dust the earth's forests, demineralized
 soil says a prayer then drinks up

Ghosts of dead cattle call out for soybean seeds, the fastfood ballgame
     is down to its last out
Awake, awake, the melody of those yearning for love can now
     continue until the next comet falls

——♀——

38

—Did you hear rumors through the years about
your brothers or your sisters?
—We were checking. There were organizations
we could go and check. Then when I went to
Israel to bring Anna over, then again
I went to an office to find my cousins.
And I went to look for my brothers.
Because I thought my brother was such an
organizer. He was a fighter. So
I went to look for my brothers. And I found
the same name, my cousins, Alta and Mandy.
My father's brother's kids had the same name,
and we found them in Jerusalem.
—Did the pain of the memories come up
often through the years? And how did you
deal with it?
—Well, I couldn't talk about it for
about 40 years. Till about five years
ago, I couldn't even talk about it.
You know that. Just a little bit I said.
When they asked me to go to speak in schools

here and there, I couldn't even talk about
it. The first time I spoke was about five
years ago in the local high school. Then
when I spoke about it, I said to the kids:
I probably was your age. I wasn't
any older than you and I went so
much through life and therefore please get your
education. Because that's very
important, and then you'll know that human
beings have to love each other, not hate.
—So, for forty years you tried not to think
about it too much?
—That's right. I thought about it. We had dreams.
Many times we woke up.
—You woke up sometimes in the middle of
the night?
—Yes, sure, lots of times, lots of times.
—Now does it help you feel better to talk
about it?
—That's right. I feel better when I talk
about it. And I hope that people, the
way I talk, should never come to this
situation. We should never go through,
any nationality, any living
soul, should go through like that. Because this is
no good for anybody. We have to
have peace or else the whole world is . . .
—When you got out, did your friends and you talk
much about politics? Did you talk about
some of the signs to recognize so that

we would see when it's rising again: What
is fascism? Or why the Russians, who
were allies during the war, became enemies
of the United States with the Cold War soon
after the war was over?
—The Russian politics was never good,
because our father was captured during
World War I in Russia. All the Jewish
people were in a little shtetel, a
little town, like here, a little village.
He had a very good voice since he was
a cantor. He used to go up on the trees
singing for all the neighbors for this whole
village, all kinds of songs, Russian too, because
he was there four years in prison.
—Your father, your father was in prison?
—A prisoner of war, four years in Russia.
Then the people in Russia were very
good but the politicians were not.
They tried to kill Jews. Because of his
beautiful voice they let him live. When they
heard my father's voice singing, they let him live.
And he had to sing for the Russian people
with the dead people around him.

39

Now, in the eurythmic imagination,
    political evolution's seedy vibrations
        are replanted
            from their most opportunistic beginnings.
It no longer matters to the epoch's skeptical eye
    why surging social democrats
        withdrew from the soapy well
            of leaderly responsibilities—
no longer matters why international cp's
    ducked under the red dictator's devouring reach
        to widen Hitler's gate
            by declaring social dems the enemy.
In this contentious dimension, archaic walls crumble,
    the Berlin armadillo down, Korean swept over with fine dirt,
        the Great Wall grizzly napping happily upon a pillow
            of a million uncensored interpretations.
In this silvery time frame, slitthroat Stalin never arose,
    no Maoist forced mass-cultured migrations,
        no bloodsoaked Khmer Rouge gravitational fields—
            actually existing socialism nowhere to be found!
On the samizdat cushions of poetic simulation
    we can ride free
        of instrumental traffic signs
            to begin at the dream again.

Now, here, no attic dust of actually existing democracy either,
    no mercurial elections bought and paid,
        no two-party bully pulpit winner-take-all
        congress of lessers

no more antimissile missile displacement
of life's unbuttery menu of nutritious necessities,
no more handheld computerized triggers
causing bloodless street corner death,
no constructing underground crutches for contra-indicated
Savimbis and Shahs. No cleanshaven dictators labeled
emerging democratic because their deathsquad pen names
are inked in the NSA checkbook.
No more thick denial-filled skulls & laser stun guns guarding
the public information safe. No more oxygenated indoctrination
techniques so subtle we don't even feel
our wet cement shoes hardening.
No more business's multinational vulture boards
pecking out the ecologic eyes of our time.
Now the terrifying transoceanic Cold War monster
is once more unborn!

Sophie Scholl, student cofounder of White Rose resistance,
awaiting the Nazi firing squad, exclaimed with diamond defiance:
"what we have written and said is in the minds of you all,
but you lack the courage to say it aloud."
A common holocaust survivor's refractive refrain:
To understand you have to go through it—
you cannot ever understand
yet you must understand.
The multiple contradictions and cataclysmic voices
are unresolveable. Memory's radical eyes never sleep.
A century after slavery declared dead
slaves still lie awake

with imperishable nightmares below deck.
　　　American Indians still see brothers & sisters falling
　　　　　along the trail of slaughtered tears.
　　　　　　　Oven smoke still stings the open eye.
Personal illustrations of bone-thin survival
　　　spread Compassion's catenated shadows
　　　　　that both heal & amplify
　　　　　　　the elastic ache of family loss.
The simplest integers don't add up:
　　　carnage's advanced technology and heartless roots
　　　　　difficult to comprehend—
　　　　　　　one likes to think everyone
has moral nuggets at their deepest core.
　　　These four nighttime headache remedies for the next century:
　　　　　recall, speak up, raise consciousness,
　　　　　　　and organize movements
to send the world toward an international
　　　egalitarian democracy
　　　　　with respect for ecology &
　　　　　　　every single human on the planet.

—that's cool doc exactly what now?

—1994 — 97

AT THE END OF THE CENTURY

—written for Allen Ginsberg at his 70th birthday

Ah century that has embraced me these past 39 years, that has set before my eyes so much tumult and catastrophe, that has taken too many of my friends and ravaged the calendar with my mother's mother's blood, that has wormed a hole

from earth's core through ozone layer to the sun, I have but one wish for you: Die my century! why wait? early to bed with you! Take early retirement, take your granite eyes, your fully paid tombstone, your electrified casket, your four billion odes to death,

burn your damn books those dastardly lies, lay your plutonium shroud over leftover legacy, let's be done with you. Artists around here in all watercolors have prefigured many paths to follow—choose one: no-warning aneurism during peaceful sleep, drunken

liver rot, kidney explosion at top of donor wait list, youthful breast cancer, no-holds-barred immune system surrender, sudden leap off college dormitory roof—if you don't like local Jersey methods, why not blow your brains out

like Russia's Mayakovsky, you betrayed his dreams as much as any-one's, over & over & over, so go ahead, straight to your grave, die my century! It's your time, the signs all there, all 500 TV channels are screaming bloody random murder,

—"Lester Leaps In" now playing on my CD, these the jazz rhythms A.G. had in mind while writing angelic "Howl," while swinging for the century's fences, ah Allen's 70th birthday last week, maybe the books are worth

saving from the bonfire, maybe some 20th century visions to carry, some ways to connect—maybe, my century, you never intended to fuck us up? Maybe never intended to walk into the bar wearing the death mask? Whatever your intentions, you're through!

Die my century, we're growing impatient, no need to prolong this multiperspectival agony, leave now so rebirth may arrive soon, too many cannot afford to wait—Goldie's kidneys can't take it much longer, you've already killed her, what more do you want?

For her, there was too much apartheid far & near, too many youth shot, too many communities allowed to go broke, too many phar-maceutical giants allowed to roughshod concrete boots through city's historic gardens—for Mark, too many fathers

dying ridiculous wars, too many mothers scrambling for shelter, too many hungry children deserving songs of their own—Audrey's landlord never let her pick up her clothes, robbery by the propertied class plain and simple, an old-fashioned crime

your courts never learned to solve—what good were you? Your patriarchal capitalisms grew immeasurable tumors, you threw out socialized medicine before inventing an alternate cure, Ethan leapt off the balcony & nobody knows why, too many too manys, cover that body, cover that experimental beard, hide that loud music, cover cover cover blood blood blood cover—now I've got this throbbing headache, like a hammer at the back of the head banging from the inside, could be sinus

infection, how am i supposed to be sure when no doctor will see anyone for days—southern black churches are burning, Woodbridge's fiery oil storage tanks at this very moment spewing huge toxic clouds, hawks drop Mideast bombs on infant ribs,

FBI looks up the wrong files, Vietnam's lessons & veterans remain locked outside our nation's checkbook memory, celebrities endorse sexy underwear sewn by starved Guatemala teens, Nigeria is hanging its writers, Philadelphia prefers to lethally inject—

how beautiful Lester's rhythms of earthly engagement, dead friends' divine energies digging those sounds, they lived spread out & diverse, they lived this century as well as died it, they rode the universe's internationalist intergenerational bus along

your potholed highways & loved outloud many of your bumpy struggles—My beloved pillowcase century! After yr breathing has slowed, we who endure will send our compassionate imaginations ahead, will keep our coalitions together with tough new thread,

our desire for change will survive the most callous assassins, so send yr ss back to their self-made hells, toss torturers East & West back into their flesh-eating ditches—let go yr thousand demons & yr one gods, merciful death & even more merciful rebirth,

we will encounter a future, the fourway mirror will forgive, eman-
cipatory eyedrops will relieve the ache, after the sliding back & the spi-
raling forth, the planet & the plan, after the redwood keyboard & the
meditative sprint, the bacbacbac back back

bacbacbac—sometime next century our sketches will come to life . . .

—1996